PLANTING ACORNS

PLANTING ACORNS

How to give your city child a country childhood

GERALDINE TAYLOR
with additional material by
Keith Taylor

i

IMPACT BOOKS

First published in Great Britain 1986
by Impact Books
112 Bolingbroke Grove, London SW11 1DA

© Geraldine Taylor

British Library Cataloguing in Publication Data

Taylor, Geraldine
  Planting acorns : how to give your city child a country childhood
  1. Natural history — Great Britain   2. Urban fauna — Great Britain   3. Urban flora —
  Great Britain
  I. Title   II. Taylor, Keith
  508.41   QH137

ISBN 0-245-54389-9

Printed and bound in Great Britain by
Biddles Ltd, Guildford and King's Lynn

'What you do in the Nature magazine, and your adventures with wildlife is very exciting: you show people what can be done now – even in the middle of a city!'
Caroline Weaver, BBC Natural History Unit (Producer of *Greenpeace – Commandos of Conservation*)

'We live in a society where ugliness is fashionable. Apart from young people like yourself, Peter, we are unfortunately breeding a race of people who can use a computer, beam messages through space, and land on other planets. But we have forgotten how to look at a blade of grass – or a wren's wing, or the bark of a tree.
May life sing in you.'
Len Baker (*Swan Rescue*)

To the memory of
Dr Mark Smith, of the University of Bristol Botanic Garden:
Botanist Extraordinary.

ACKNOWLEDGEMENTS

We would like to acknowledge, with deepest gratitude, those who have so generously given permission to reproduce extracts from correspondence and articles written for *Eye on Local Nature*:

Bridget Smith – for permission to publish Dr Mark Smith's letters and articles, Heather and Robin Tanner, Derwent May, Dr Michael Crawley, Dr John Brierley, Caroline Weaver, Len Baker, John Waldon, Trevor Baker, Alix Lord, Emma Emms, Martin Rogers, Jennifer Veale.

Thank you, also, to all those contributors and readers who have taken the boys' magazine to their hearts and given it such loyal support. And to Jean-Luc Barbanneau for helping us to tell the story.

All illustrations, unless otherwise acknowledged in the text, are by Peter Taylor.

Geraldine and Keith Taylor

Contents

Part one
IN SEARCH

Up the clump

I fell in love with the countryside ten years after I abandoned it to live in the middle of a city with its brick walls and welcomed distractions. I'm told – a little too often, I feel, that I was a sullen child and teenager. But our family life was sad and often bizarre. My poor mother was becoming more and more paralysed by multiple sclerosis and I found it impossible to face the fact that there would be no cure.

The Kent countryside around us – Nurstead, Southfleet, Meopham, was classically lovely, but the effect of all this beauty on me was unbearable: it was an insult to my mother's suffering. My most precious photograph is of my mother as I never knew her. It shows a bold, athletic girl on a sports bike, laughing at the camera (and my father who took the picture) as she flaunted her long, perfectly formed legs in the briefest of cycling shorts. No wonder my father was so much in love with her. But by the time I was five, mum could no longer wander in fields and lanes and later, even car journeys (with me holding her head straight, or with her head forced upright by a stick and an elastic garter – which worked up and sprung off every few minutes) were nightmares of tension. What was the point of all the beauty of the countryside? It refused to grieve with me and I could have taken a flamethrower to every inch of it.

I'm telling this simply to explain that when, years later, I began to explore the country for the sake of my son and as a hobby for my own family, I was in the same position as most novices: probably in a worse position. How many novices would bring that much resentment and hostility with them!

Yet, I suppose my country childhood had forcibly taught me how to lose myself without organised entertainment – and I had learned from experience when and where to locate wild flowers. For certain patches of those flowers, especially the early-blossoming violets, I formed proprietary attachments. From January onwards I mounted guard on them, looking at the plants and at the ground around them, willing each bud to colour and open. They *had* to hurry up. I needed them.

When the plants flowered, I picked them for my mother, mechani-

3

cally stripping whole patches. Although the prospect of offering these in abundance was always clouded by the knowledge that mum could never see them growing, they seemed to have more to offer her than garden flowers – so I ruthlessly scoured the local woodlands in search of fresh supplies. These flowers were my passport to short times without guilt. Multiple sclerosis had begun its hateful, crippling grasp on my mother in the months after my birth. Mum often told me she could never entirely forgive me. With that much suffering, only a saint could have avoided blaming – but mum could have saved her breath. I have never forgiven myself.

So I knew where to find flowers. I also had time to devote to the finding of 'lucky' four-leaved clovers and while these, offered daily in the summer and wished on, couldn't cure the disease any more than the chicken wishbone proffered at Christmas, the four-leaved clover skill proved useful many years later.

Let me explain. The apparent luck in finding them is actually a mixture of trance-like concentration, sufficient desperation and a faith in the existence of the unusual. You have to believe they are there if you want to find them. I soon discovered that if a plant yields one lucky clover, it will usually have others – but this 'magic' born of observation and logic was always in demand.

This was a skill I went on practising for my son Peter's amusement when he was a toddler and I took him to our local parks. But for Peter, of course, I'd have stayed safely within the city and walked on pavements all my life. Certainly, I'd have kept away from anything green. But, like most conscientious mums, I did my bit of park visiting, expressing vague interest in birds and sometimes trying to find something appreciative to say about trees. I noticed that some parents looked as if they were enjoying their time in the park – but I reasoned that they were better at pretending than I was. Looking back from an extremely safe distance, I can see that life with a pre-school child can be peculiar. At the time I accepted its ad hoc nature and blamed my feelings of disorientation on my own inability to adjust from the disciplines of working life. Anyway, that's when an unusual couple came into our lives for a while and gave me a glimpse of another existence.

A sullen, withdrawn child joined the playgroup I helped to run. The little boy refused to speak to the adult helpers. Peter took a half bottle of milk and a box of lego over to him and sat with him for a while. The little boy wouldn't speak to Peter either. None of us knew quite what to do. We wondered if the child could speak. I suggested we leave him for a bit to find his feet and asked Peter to play with him now and then. I left playgroup late as usual, after tidying up and making sure all the children had been collected. Peter and I locked the church hall and walked into the yard – and found the little boy waiting for us – pointing at Peter and waving to a man I took to be his father.

Thomas, a tall, fair Frenchman in his late twenties didn't beat about the bush. 'My son likes your son. Will you be friends with us?' And so, for a time, we were. Thomas was out of work and Carole, his English wife, a qualified doctor and as silent as her son, made a living for them working part-time on the local blood donor units. She was pregnant again. They were very poor – and their flat was unhealthily damp and cold. Thomas collected firewood several times a week to fuel their open fire and he would usually call on me to see if I would bring Peter to the woods with him to play with his son Johnny. It was awkward – Peter found the silent Johnny an impossible playmate and it's hard to explain to a four-year old that when people ask for your friendship, they need it.

Thomas made an event out of collecting the firewood – he'd pretend to put the two boys into his sack and throw twigs high into the air for them to catch. Then, one day – on a beautiful autumn afternoon, he put down his sack of wood, collected some fallen leaves and called Johnny to him. Peter and I watched while Thomas held these leaves against the sun and showed Johnny the patterns of the veins and the different colours – the green, the yellow, the red. Johnny's face lit up like the leaves in a smile I'd never seen before. Father and son became so close – the affection was so tangible – that Peter and I felt intruders. Johnny relapsed into his usual silent self as we walked on. 'That was a moment of wonder', Thomas explained to me. I could see it was – I could also see that those feelings and appreciation, were at that time, far beyond my reach.

Soon after this Keith and I found ourselves at odds with the sheer speed and expense of city life. In a city like Bristol, there are so many events, entertainments, places to see. Good times were organised so quickly that they seemed discarded almost as they drew to an end. Dismissal and anticipation occupied the same breath. Where was the time to relish? It was getting to feel like a roller coaster.

The science fiction cult was beginning to affect the toy shops – there was considerable pressure to buy Superhero toys and clothes and books. I wasn't earning a high salary as I'd made 'fitting in' round

Peter's playgroup and later his school hours a priority. Keith had entered accountancy in his twenties and his salary wasn't all that high either. We had become irritable and worried about money. And very restless.

There had to be more to life than the next purchase. Logical as ever, I decided that the next time Peter showed an interest in something more spiritual than his bike, I'd commit myself to encouraging this interest in depth – whatever it was.

Like most six-year-olds, Peter was an eager reader of Nature stories and books about animals and the country. Whenever asked what his interests were, Peter would doggedly reply, 'My bike and Nature'. It might not last, I thought, but it'll do for the time being. And so I committed myself to slowing down our city life by helping Peter to develop his interest in Nature. I would take him from books to the reality – and see if he loved that! We would start on a small scale – but it goes without saying that we had no garden to our small flat. Step one was to 'find' a garden. We decided to 'adopt' a clump of the Bristol Downs as our own – and see how it went from there . . .

There was no point waiting. We started in the bleakest winter, in December, long before any leaves had appeared on the trees or any shoots (that we could notice) were coming through the ground. It was very, very cold. We chose to look for our clump along the wildish track of parkland which skirts the Downs opposite Bristol Zoo. Trousers and sensible shoes formed no part of my wardrobe in those days, so, unsuitably dressed and cursing, we scrambled through vicious brambles to the middle of a well-hidden clump of oak and birch trees. It looked quite promising – a little wood within comforting reach of civilization. We sat down, the three of us. Peter full of hope, Keith believing this was a reasonable way of keeping away from the shops and the temptation to overspend every Saturday, and I, feeling hungry already.

Nothing happened. We looked around us, felt foolish when a family passed us on their way to the zoo and peered in, and realised how long ten minutes was. We had agreed to stay twenty. Then, to my great relief, a robin started to circle us, getting nearer, and bolder, leaning his head to one side to get a closer look. Attempts to follow his movements by shifting our bodies were counter-productive and we had to stay still and silent if we wanted the robin to stay with us. But this was enough to justify this first mission. The clump became ours, complete with what we hoped was a resident robin.

Visits to the clump became the focus of Saturday and Sunday mornings, despite the relentlessly cold, wet weather. It was a horrible winter. Our robin always appeared for us and we soon learned to make the waiting more bearable by packing a flask of tea and packets of biscuits. Once he was used to us, the robin flew to us quickly, however much we whispered, moved about to avoid cramp and passed the thermos. While we were sitting there, too, we little by little relaxed enough to look around and wonder what the berries, leaves and interesting humps of earth were all about. Peter formulated intriguing and wonderfully erroneous theories about what we saw. Everything was rare – and the mounds of earth were testaments to unusual animal life under the earth! I think we were fortunate not to have many facts about our surroundings as these extravagant theories were part of the growing charm of our own little woodland.

When we were sitting in the clump, we had to remind each other not to talk about anything but the woodland – so there were lots of silences. I believe that's how the atmosphere of the woods began its magic seduction. We learned to look about us, look at the detail, look beyond looking – and to keep the world at bay in our thoughts.

We decided to spend our Christmas morning up the clump with the robin – and for the first time he did not turn up! Disappointed, we sung carols out of tune in the middle of the wood to remind the robin that we were in the clump. Sure enough, the robin appeared on Boxing day, in company with several squirrels. We regard any 'furry life' as a bonus!

I always expect spring to begin on January the first and realised now just how long it does take. However, as the weather warmed and the sun shone, each new shoot, bud and flower was a special present for us. Having greeted the robin, we wandered farther afield and found patches of huge white violets, glossy celandines with satin petals, snow-white barren strawberry – and later, miraculously, even a small patch of wood anemones flowered in the clump itself – at first mistaken by me for a white tissue, thrown away.

Every time we went up the clump something new awaited us: a different bird or flower – or a different shade of the same flower. Surely, we thought, there were different sorts of violets. Some smell and are chunky, and there are others with no scent but with a paler colour and more delicate shape. We needed a book to tell us. We began to notice insects, especially the enchanting little furry beefly with its snout and proboscis, visiting our clump violets like a miniature brown hummingbird spotlighted in the shafts of sunlight.

Peter made a map of the clump with appropriate labels – Robin Wood, Violet Patch, Squirrel Tree, Magpie Clearing – and we called the areas by these names rather than the previous 'That bit opposite the zoo gates' or 'The part round from the mud patch'.

Apart from this, we were not yet keeping records of what we saw, but I begun to use a child's paintbox to paint the flowers and date each painting. My early efforts at watercolours are awful – clumsy and inaccurate – but I improved simply by making myself look more closely at the flowers, how they were formed, and watching them move and respond to the slightest breeze, even to my breath. I expected to be able to predict the appearance of these flowers the following year from the date I had written, and this was how we learned that flowers do not always appear in the same week each year – or even in the same month!

Written records started to mark an emotional rather than a factual event. Peter and I usually went up the clump after school to greet the robin, eat sandwiches and look for birds. One evening the robin did not appear. We waited for an hour and then I stood up to go – and noticed that there was a pile of feathers in the bush. We drew them out and examined them. They were rust coloured – like the breast of our robin – and they were blood-stained and ragged. We sat down again and waited, still hoping for the best.

Forced home by the coming darkness, I recorded in my diary that we thought the clump robin had been killed. I believed that the special happiness we had found up the clump was so vulnerable that it was bound to end this way. I counted up that we had had five months of happiness 'with Nature'. That seemed reasonable enough. I never trusted it anyway.

As it turned out, the magic was not as frail as I thought – and this was to be the first of many wrong conclusions! The robin arrived, intact, on our visit to show Keith its last feathered remains. This time, Peter wrote in *his* diary that the clump robin had come back in one piece!

After this, I started to record. I wrote down the budding of each species of flower and the different birds and butterflies we could identify. By now, we were seeing birds we'd never previously noticed – long-tailed tits, bullfinches, goldcrests, dunnocks. When there was too much to put into my diary along with dentist appointments and birthdays, I started to use a separate hardback notebook.

I wonder why we record? I was trying to hold on to what I'd seen to prolong the happiness, probably to prove it had actually happened. It was good to look back on, too. In his own good time, Peter became curious about my recordings and paintings and wanted to join in both activities.

Without some reference books, we wouldn't have known what we were recording, so after four or five months we had built up a small library of books about flowers and birds. We already owned the immensely useful *AA Book of the British Countryside* and to this we added the Reader's Digest *Wild Flowers of Britain* and the Reader's Digest *Birds of Britain*. Experienced naturalists will probably wince at these choices – but experienced naturalists have no reason to read this account! All three of these books are hypnotically absorbing. Even Peter curled up in bed with the flower book, night upon night, and became enthralled by the herbal histories of each plant. The books, read for pleasure as well as identification, gave us ideas for plants and birds to look out for. We began to long to see certain birds – like the treecreeper or the nuthatch – and would go in search of them, with a record of success which astounded us! Similarly, we would set off to track down as yet unseen wild flowers with the same tenacity. Even I had to concede there might be something in this Nature business . . .

FIND A CLUMP!

Everywhere I go I see little clumps similar to ours – even in central London! I've just found an ideal clump in Camden Gardens.

☐ Our pact to have a few minutes silent observation was the key to all our future involvement. We agreed on this before we went and largely stuck to it. If you take an adult friend, make sure he or she is sympathetic to the idea. I've had trips ruined by friends who talk too much!

☐ No need for special clothing – wear what you usually wear outdoors and take something to sit on, like an old mac or a groundsheet.

☐ A clump is best with bushes and trees – it will be a little more secluded and the bushes provide cover for the wild birds. Trees mean you might see squirrels and some of the shyer birds.

☐ It's best to sit down when you get there – you'll be less conspicuous and your eyes will be nearer the ground to see flowers and insects.

☐ There's no need to be silent all the time – just quiet – and don't make any sudden movements.

☐ Food and drink helps to relax you and keep everyone good-humoured. In the winter it can be a lifesaver!

☐ This isn't *work*! Try leaving all recording and identification books at home. Look really hard at your new discoveries so that you can look them up when you get back. This way you will remember where they were – and you'll want to go back to check your identification was correct.

☐ Morning clump visits are best to start with. There are fewer people about (especially on Saturday mornings when everyone else is in the shops) and a lot less disturbance. Some summer flowers work part-time and shut in the afternoon! In winter, too, it gets dark and cold very quickly after lunchtime.

☐ If you choose a clump you can walk to, you can visit it regularly, as we did, throughout the seasons. I found clump visiting marvellous in the school holidays – it gave us a daily focus and interest. And it was completely free!

☐ On your first visit with the children, look out for a robin . . .

Farther afield

Our Nature trips started in the winter of 1979. At first we couldn't bear to spend any more than two hours out in the cold and wet weather, preferring to go out in the morning – falling darkness is creepy for wood visitors! In the beginning, too, it mattered to us to have somewhere to aim for – first the clump and later, other hideouts and landmarks. Glades, large misshapen trees, rocks and banks were adopted and given our special names. We always set off with a 'mission' such as to see if *any* celandines were out yet, to see if the clump anemone shoots had broken through the earth – or to see if we could catch just one more glimpse of the elusive green woodpecker who lived and laughed at us near the zoo.

We never abandoned the clump, but by the following winter, we were also travelling farther afield, cycling over the Clifton Suspension Bridge to the slopes of the Ashton Court Estate (a huge, part-wooded, hilly park) and to the mysterious Leigh Woods high above the Avon Gorge cliffs.

We learned what made this kind of trip bearable: we had to learn a lot, in fact, because we committed ourselves to a family motto, 'We go anyway . . . '. Whatever the weather. One trip, in spectacularly stormy weather, culminated in a huge branch of the very tree under which we were sheltering crashing down inches from our heads. On another occasion, we could feel – and see – the Clifton Suspension Bridge swaying horribly under our feet as we braved the high winds to get home. I thought I was going to be blown off and die and was sickly green for hours afterwards. But this kind of experience made a good story. Never before an 'outdoor' type, I hadn't realised that conditions in this country could be so extreme. We often felt like Arctic explorers and several times I found myself crying with cold.

To make our 'go anyway' resolve feasible and less irresponsible, we each built up a collection of bad weather kit – layers of warm jumpers (shetland is good), waterproof coats, plastic over-trousers, two pairs of gloves (wet woolly gloves are particularly vile), walking boots – and woolly hats. Getting cold through and through and being miles from home is frightening. I, of course, was the last to realise that no one would laugh at me in my full over-trousers and big boots outfit – and that anyway, what did it matter if they did? At last I realised that however wet we were, we could be changed and dry in ten minutes at home, and that all mud can be contained and removed. Previously, I think I'd regarded mud as corrosive! We even turned getting muddy to advantage by having a 'muddiest bum' competition when one of us had fallen in a large puddle.

After ten minutes of fresh air, I'm ravenous. We needed more and more food. Keith began to carry a stout rucksack packed with cheese rolls, Garibaldi biscuits (good on stodge) and apples – and a giant thermos of tea. There was also room in the rucksack for a groundsheet, although for some reason this irritates me, and I'd rather perch on a tree-stump or sit on wet grass.

Once we'd started to overcome the problem of keeping warm and adequately dry in the harshest weather (and shaded in the summer – because, believe it or not, it can be relentlessly hot!) we discovered that every season has much to offer. Once spring starts in earnest, it's like a race – it's hard to keep up with each new discovery – there's almost too much to see, smell, touch and hear. Summer seems drab by comparison, and the pleasures of autumn are perhaps better understood.

Winter is an acquired taste and we came to love it by looking for detail. After the blackberries withered in the autumn, we looked for the intricate dried skeletons of summer wild flowers, for seed-cases and seeds, for ferns, moss, lichen and berries – and for the late autumn fungi with all their brilliantly varied camouflage and atmosphere of danger . . .

And what gruesome and sinister names fungi have earned! Beechwood sickener, poison pie, ugly milk-cap, amethyst deceiver, witches' butter, death cap, destroying angel. We regarded all fungi as potentially lethal (some are, of course), and Keith constantly reminded Peter and me to wash our hands after holding them – or if we were still in the wood, to pass round the food without touching it with our fingers! Roger Phillips' *Mushrooms* (Pan) is a marvellous, photographic guide to fungi, ideal for identification in the woods and even better for tantalising dark-evening winter reading at home. Peter and I often speculate on how some of the names were awarded!

Some flowers bloom on past late autumn and when we found plants flowering out of the season specified for them by the textbooks, we realised that Nature does not always act predictably and on cue. Anything might happen! And *we* might be the ones to discover it! Peter and I searched the Avon Gorge for the very last flowering rockrose (a dainty, tissue-paper-like yellow flower) and found one in bloom on the first day of December. The following year we discovered a common violet in late October, huddling next to a fallen pine-cone.

Even though I get colder and hungrier than Peter and Keith, the winter months became my favourites. Winter is the perfect time to walk through the woods absorbing the full atmosphere. This atmosphere became a compulsion for me – detaining me despite freezing fingers and throbbing ears, calling me back week after week to the darkest parts of Leigh Woods. Dire things have happened in Leigh Woods, according to Bristolians who as a result give them a wide berth. Factually, there have been 'incidents' – and rumours of others – in the past. It's safe enough there now. Part of it is owned by the National Trust and part by the Forestry Commission. Objectively, I suppose some of it is creepy if you fear being alone in a wood. When you lose that fear, there's nothing like it.

In the winter, in Leigh Woods, we saw few people. Isolation is part of the intense, alien atmosphere and our conversation tended to dwindle to nothing as we looked beyond looking at what was happening to the woodland floor, to those leaves which remained, and to the quiet, waiting trees. During our first winter of observation, Peter and I strained our eyes to look for all the colour we could find in the woods – and in this way we focused on detail and pattern.

But winter is also the time for learning the woods, for getting bearings, for mapping the paths – or committing them to memory – and for testing instincts for direction. Woods look quite different – much more confusing – when they are in full or even partial foliage. And along the pathways, leaves of some plants remain. We noted where the patches of frail white wood-sorrel, violets and perky four-petalled tormentil would be in the spring. By wandering through parts of the wood which would be overgrown and inaccessible in summer, we found badger holes – and huge setts with up to 17 holes – and discovered the hairs, fresh earth diggings, dung pits and snuffle holes (where badgers have snuffled around grubbing for food) which prove the setts to be occupied! A visit to the setts in the rapidly melting snow (it was a race against time to get there before the light snow covering disappeared) showed us badger footprints around the holes and leading off along the many tiny badger paths. These badger paths are narrower than human paths and wind under fallen branches. These paths took us from one dark yew tree to another (badgers love yew berries), past many scratching trees – trees with their bases deeply gored – often gouged white where the badgers sharpen or clean their claws. Or simply scratch for pleasure. Experts don't really know why they scratch! We started to long to actually *see* a badger.

Birds are easier to see when the leaves are not fully covering the trees, and, at some stage on each midwinter walk, we were surrounded by a travelling party of blue tits, great tits, long-tailed tits and goldcrests. These congregated loudly around the top of the conifers for a few minutes and then moved on. It was easier to see nuthatches, treecreepers and wrens as winter turned to early spring and the birds become more and more active. Of course, the much loved robins are always nearby – and usually serenaded our picnics.

I found that individual bird song is more easily picked out in the winter because fewer birds are singing. Peter and I learned to identify robin, blackbird, dunnock, wren and thrush first of all – and soon came to be able to recognise the calls of the bullfinch, tits and goldcrest.

As winter finally ends, the mating birds are at their loudest, most colourful – and reckless. They are usually so intent on their courtship that they take no notice of us observing them. Before the leaves conceal their nesting activities, there's a wonderland of nest-building to watch. We bought two pairs of binoculars and for the first time were enchanted by the sheer irridescent beauty of the birds – and the thrill of seeing their beaks open in the song we were hearing.

Binoculars need persistence. We are still trying to acquire the birdwatcher's skill of using them to actually locate birds not first spotted by eye. We tend to look first without binoculars and then use them to focus on what we see. I'm reassured, though, by the experienced birdwatchers who have told me (in strictest confidence – this is quite an admission) that this is still their method.

There is plant life in January! At least, in the Bristol area. We have January sweet violets (the chunky, dark mauve or white scented ones), sometimes celandines and leaves of cuckoo-pint, dog's mercury and the peculiar (is it or isn't it ugly? – is the smell nice or sickly?) winter heliotrope.

Every year, though, desperation mounts as our longing for spring flowers heightens. This craving made us look all the more intently and we were rewarded by finding the vigorous – and rare – green helle-

14

bore. This looks like the devil or an angel depending on one's mood. But its sheer life and force at a time when other plants are dormant is haunting. Less rare but just as welcome was our first breathtaking discovery of the lime-green trumpet flowers of the spurge laurel on the slopes of the Avon Gorge.

As well as my small amount of written recording, we were always impatient to find out more detail about what we had seen – and to check if it really was the 'rarity' our wild guesses had proclaimed it to be. If a plant or a bird was new to us, it was rare until proven otherwise – as it almost invariably was! I found it useful to write a few pencil details in my notebook to help us with reference book identification when we returned home. For birds, I recorded the size in comparison with a common bird like a sparrow or blackbird; the colouring; where it was and what it was doing. A typical record would be: 'Smaller than sparrow. Green/Light-brown (blur), flitting quickly in branches of conifer. High up.' I'd try to mention something about the song and Peter was better than I was at picking out and describing individual song. I'd write describing the song as loud, soft, melodious or repetitious.

If I was observing a plant new to us, I made a rough life-size sketch of the leaves and the flower, and recorded the colour of the petals and stamens and commented on the scent, if any. It took us several years to come to grips with tree and shrub identification. I think plants and birds are our special love.

Attempted identification took place immediately we got home and, if the trip had been in the rain, we would stomp around the flat, half-dressed, our clothes steaming, in the process of getting dry, drinking tomato soup and trying to track down what we had seen in our growing library of reference books.

By our second year of observation, this small library included:
Wild Flowers of Britain, Roger Phillips (Ward Lock/Pan).
Mushrooms, Roger Phillips (Pan).
Grasses, Ferns, Mosses & Lichens, Roger Phillips (Pan).
The Tree Key, Herbert Edlin (Warne).
The Roger Phillips guides, illustrated entirely by photographs are excellent for identification because they show actual (and occasionally tatty) specimens such as we were finding at first. Painted illustrations, while lovely to pore over, can be rather idealised representations of the plants and, as beginners, we found the realism of photography preferable. Later, though, we discovered where to find flowers which

outshone the paintings in their profusion and splendour! We also realised that each stage of the plant – from seed-leaf or new shoot – to seed-case and seed has a mystery and intricacy of its own. One stage will find the deepest place in our hearts. Peter loves the fully-opened flower and I am most drawn to the very earliest leaves.

It was nearly two years since I acted on Peter's expressed love of Nature and it was obvious to us all that my own yearnings were the reason why we spent so much of our weekends sitting in the clump or the woods. I was reaching out for an appreciation of beauty which could be felt with the emotions as well as seen by the eyes. Others could feel this and I envied them. Book or television knowledge was not enough. It hasn't got the feeling – the love. This love is not the sum of knowledge of the kind which can put appropriate labels on the right bird or plant. It's the love which grows from a strange kind of companionship. From being with the plants, the birds, the trees and the flowers in all weathers, knowing where they are as well as what man has chosen to call them – and from being able to know a little of how they are faring at each stage of their vulnerable lives.

My seduction by the dreaded 'Nature' was complete. When I find an island of primroses in the ocean of fallen beech leaves, or a tiny tormentil along a pathside, I feel as helpless with love as when I see a babyhood photograph of Peter or come across his first written letters to us. I want to protect and watch over. It is exactly the same feeling of love.

VENTURING FARTHER

Mild in climate as the West Country is reputed to be, in the last ten years temperatures as high as 33.8°C (93°F) and as low as −12.8°C (9°F) have been recorded! Venturing farther afield is a more adventurous and more hazardous business – and we acknowledged the need to be better equipped for all weather conditions.

☐ Good clothing is essential in coping with the elements – but it doesn't have to be expensive; in fact, the older the better. We wear a ragbag of old hiking and army surplus gear. What matters is that the clothing must be waterproof and warm – and thornproof (splinters!). These are our essentials:

ANORAK I use a light nylon PVC-lined anorak and Keith wears and old padded motorcycle jacket with a zipped front. This can be opened up when it gets hot – without having to be taken off – and this matters if you are the one carrying the rucksack! As for Peter, now that he's a teenager, he's somewhat image conscious and wears a cotton combat jacket. Pride seems to keep him warm, but I carry an extra anorak just in case.

TROUSERS We all wear loose fitting cotton jeans which are comfortable and thorn resistant. However, if these get wet – or are too tight, they cling to your legs and you will lose body heat at an alarming rate. We keep our legs dry with light-weight nylon over-trousers.

SPARE PULLOVER We always take a spare pullover with us in case one of our party suddenly feels cold. Actually this can happen at any time of the year if a sudden downpour is followed by a strong, cold wind. Exposure can set in – and it's vital to be able to act quickly (see Appendix Three on 'Toughening up').

BUSH HAT A broad-brimmed 'explorer' hat can be bought cheaply from most army surplus stores. We wear them in the summer to keep the sun off our heads, back of our necks – and eyes. They have their uses in wet weather too – to keep the rain from running down the back of the neck. However, in high winds they take to the air, and Keith is forever losing his over the Clifton Suspension Bridge! A woolly ski hat is better in the winter.

BOOTS In the summer, Peter and I wear trainers because these grip better on rock faces. But in the winter we wear heavy walking boots with commando pattern soles. Gumboots are not especially suitable as they are freezing cold in winter, hellish to get on and off, and nasty to walk long distances in. Boots, with oversocks are warmer, grip better in the mud and offer ankle protection when crossing rough slopes.

GLOVES Having ruined many pairs of woollen gloves, I acknowledge the usefulness of cheap, loose fitting vinyl or leather gloves. These are waterproof and give protection for the hands when fighting through dense brambles or overgrown paths – and when it's very cold, another pair of woolly gloves can go inside them.

DOUBLING-UP In the worst weather, usually January and February, we stay warm by wearing two of everything – even old pyjama bottoms inside jeans if necessary. Remember that our motto was 'We go anyway . . .'

☐ As we began to pursue our different preoccupations in greater depth, some equipment was necessary:

BINOCULARS We bought two pairs of fairly cheap 8 × 30 binoculars. These magnify everything eight times, so the effect is that of being eight times closer than we are! These became part of bird watching – especially at nesting time. They also bring butterflies enchantingly closer – and I've even located flowers up rock faces this way!

CAMERAS Peter and Keith use Olympus 35 mm cameras (SLRs). Using cameras by the same manufacturer enables them (though rarely peacably!) to swop lenses and accessories. Photography is very important in observation because photographs save the need to take specimens and possibly damage rare plants (see section on photography). Photography is a thousand times preferable to the questionable pastime of pressing flowers!

COLLECTING BOX I use a small plastic box for collecting leaves, fungi and curiosities such as badger bones.

NOTEBOOK A small pocket book with stiff board covers is all I use for field recording.

☐ We split our equipment between a small shoulder bag that I carry containing items I need quick access to – such as my binoculars, collecting box and notebook, and a large rucksack which Keith nobly heaves around. This is packed with the two cameras and spare lenses – and a small ground sheet – as well as the huge thermos, sandwiches and the spare pullover. In one of his pockets, Peter carries the rudiments of an emergency kit: a map, compass and a whistle – as well as a bar of chocolate and an emergency packet of Polos (see Appendix Three on 'Toughening up').

☐ When you get into the countryside, slow down a bit. There's a lot of waiting to do and it's time to relax and let your senses take over. All the equipment in the world is nothing without our senses as hunters of mystery, beauty and the extraordinary.

☐ Once you know what is more or less usual in trips farther afield, concentrate on the unusual. Trust your instincts – listen, smell and look for what is *different*: the twig which suddenly cracks, colour among the dry leaves, the strange scent which tells that fungi is near, a leaf high up which moves when the air is still . . .

A wild flower garden

For the first time, wild flowers mattered to us and my soulless preference for concrete had been overthrown. Peter noticed the wild flowers within the city itself, flowers which squeeze up the cracks of pavements and cling precariously to the walls. Ivy-leaved toadflax is a widespread and particularly enchanting dry-stone wall flower in the west of England; the flower itself is a tiny mauve and lemon blossom – a miniature snapdragon. The concrete areas around our Bristol flat – and our own decrepit dry-stone walls housed this little flower, as well as pink herb robert, ferns, brambles – and the omnipresent self-sown hogweed.

Butterflies flew over the arrid tarmac on the way to fertile gardens. I wanted us to be surrounded by wild flowers so that these same butterflies might be tempted to stay awhile with us! Our problem was that we had no garden at all – and if I wanted to make a wild flower garden, it would have to be on the steep and rocky bank down to our basement – an unpromising scrap of land almost without topsoil.

Anyone wanting to create such a garden from scratch as I did is best forewarned that it can be at best a challenge to try to buy a very small amount of topsoil in the middle of a city: suppliers stand unyieldingly by their minimum load stipulations, expressing contempt for the idea of a town rockery. I started by telephoning garden centres and soon found that it was more productive to describe my problem to them and to ask for help – 'I'm trying to build a rockery – how do I get topsoil?' – than to starkly enquire whether or not they stocked it.

Pleas for manly advice eventually led to the telephone number of the head of a firm of haulage contractors who for some reason or other 'might be able to see you right'. Indeed he did. The gentleman concerned was so amused by my request that he offered me whatever amount of earth I wanted for the mere cost of delivery. How much did I want? I had no idea. I hopefully described the size of the area I wanted to cover and we agreed on about half a lorry load. We had forgotten to discuss the size of the lorry.

At the specified time that afternoon, a large tipper-lorry braked outside and backed up. I watched in sick panic as the lorry up-ended and a formidable wedge of earth was deposited in the driveway. £5 covered delivery and tip, but I then had to purchase a £12 shovel as none of the neighbours had one and my trowel wasn't up to the job.

The afternoon was hot and dry so there was no threat of rain robbing me of my precious topsoil – but the mountain was blocking the main way into the building for the other flat-dwellers – so I had to shift the load quickly. I stripped down to the minimum of clothing (which at least lured several men into rolling up their shirt sleeves and shifting a bit) and started to move the earth onto the bank. Passers-by were most encouraging. Peter and Keith joined in as soon as they came home and the elderly lady in the flat above handed eggs out of her window to keep our strength up. Although the earth had seemed an incredible mound, it was in fact just enough to give me an overall depth of 15–20 cm. We could have used more!

During the autumn of the year, we collected wild flower seeds from the roadsides and parts of the Bristol Downs subject to Council cropping (our clump itself is regularly under attack by 'improvement'). Peter and his friends loved 'seed sessions'. We discovered the ingenious ways in which plants store, ripen and spread their seeds. Now that we understood the relationship between flower and seed, picking became taboo.

There is fascinating variety and Heath-Robinson inventiveness in seeding! We loved poppies with their pepper-pot seed-cases and harebells with their tipping-out backwards mechanism. Foxgloves and campion seed capsules are like chock-full spice jars – and the fun with the brittle, twisty birdsfoot-trefoil pods is to catch the seeds before the cases explode in the heat of the sun and scatter their contents. Mallow seeds are like tiny maggots (I thought they *were* tiny maggots) and in high summer, it's wonderful to try to catch the billowing clouds of rosebay willowherb's plumed seeds; most of them eluded our hands as they liberated themselves high on the wind.

We always collected in dry weather (seeds can go mouldy), took only a very few seeds from each plant (and this itself delightfully prolongs the activity) and none at all from any rare or protected plant. I stored my seeds in a pillbox and in little gummed stamp-collection packets bought from the local stationers. We had no experience of germinating seeds, so we divided them into half to be sown at once, and half to sow the following spring. Peter wanted to plant some seeds at once so that he could feel the wild flower garden was on the move.

We sowed these seeds in a haphazard way, sprinkling them on top of the soil on a damp day when the wind wasn't strong enough to blow them away. I anchored some of the billowy willowherb seeds with a small stone. Peter wrote in his notebook, 'The Garden, 15th July, 1981. Today I planted ivy and quaking grass. I also planted grasses, rockroses and red campion and they will all come up soon.' He stuck a sign *Boarding House de Nature – To Let* on his patch.

Some seeds did germinate within the month and sent out leaves in the autumn. Peter wrote down the dates they first appeared and predictions as to what they were. We discovered that first leaves, from the seeds (called cotyledons) are usually quite different in shape from later leaves.

Every morning of the following (late) spring brought a different shoot or bud and eventually he was able to make exact identification. Many of the wild flowers had come in with the soil: we hadn't planted them! Buds burst into flower overnight. Peter went into competition with a friend round the corner who owned a similar little garden. Peter recorded all of these in the first year of our wild flower garden!

Flower list – 1st June 1982

lesser yellow trefoil	scarlet pimpernel
bulbous buttercups	ivy-leaved toadflax
cut-leaved cranesbill	rosebay willowherb
bush vetch	enchanter's nightshade
red valerian	birdsfoot-trefoil
salad burnet	barren strawberry
pink herb robert	clover
herb bennet	poppies
goosegrass	broad-leaved willowherb
	annual wall rocket

Miraculously, all these butterflies were tempted down, and spent time in our rockery – a few yards away from a busy main road!

speckled wood	brimstone
red admiral	comma
small tortoiseshell	peacock
painted lady	common blue

The beautiful common blue butterflies settled on the enormous patch of birdsfoot-trefoil at the base of the rockery. This is the plant on which they lay their eggs.

Between us we recorded, drew, painted and photographed these flowers and in the autumn, we were able to harvest our own seeds. Friends requested them and we became small-scale local suppliers! The following year we proudly watched mallow, foxgloves, scabious, St John's wort and harebells thrive – and their seeds were shared in turn. We cordoned off small areas for other children who wanted a garden of their own and who wanted to stake a claim in our wild flower bank. However short-lived, their interest was lovely while it lasted – and one little boy won his cub gardening badge by observing the progress of what he planted in our rockery!

It's possible to buy wild flower seeds from conservation societies and garden centres, but we had much more success with the seeds we harvested ourselves from the wild – and anyway, the seed gathering, labelling and storing is all part of the fun. We didn't introduce plants that do not normally grow in our area at all, as it's unlikely that they would flourish in a different soil. Many wild flower books go into all this – telling which flowers thrive on which soil. In Bristol, for example, we are mostly limestone. It made sense to gather from the countryside as close to home as we could. The Reader's Digest *Wild Flowers of Britain* is useful for the seed-gathering because it describes the natural habitat of the flower and the method of seeding. This can be vital with some flowers – such as herb robert – whose ingenious seed mechanism was far from obvious to us.

Of course there are disadvantages to the ownership of a wild flower garden beside the home. We were besieged by an intriguing number of creatures – snails, ladybirds, caterpillars, ants, grasshoppers, woodlice, shield bugs and vast spiders – many of which found their way indoors. Snails leave a silver trail on the fitted carpets – and we recently gently relocated a large and fat garden cross spider from our front room doorway where it had just completed its admirable web. I'm sure our wild flower garden was responsible for the wasps' nest which established itself in our dry-stone wall and caused panic among the other flat-dwellers. My assurances were ignored – I was outvoted – and a Council pest controller was summoned to kill the lot. Ugh.

Also, wild flowers take over: theirs is a strong fight for survival and they will dominate the area, banishing domestic plants. (Anyone who has done battle with hogweed or ground elder will testify to the tenacity of wild plants.) Theirs, too, can be a short flowering time and late autumn may see your garden sporting only scabious, harebells and the last of the poppies. Neighbours looked askance at our passionately wild summer excess – and scrubby autumn patch.

But those summer months are such an indescribably vivid wealth of wild flowers and insect and butterfly activity. That's enough for us! To fetch the morning paper and venture outside in bare feet to check up on the daily progress of the birdsfoot-trefoil – and see it in flower – is to believe the walls of the city diminished. And just to draw the curtains in the early morning and see the dewy scarlet of new poppies – knowing that these petals will be scattered on the winds by dusk to be replaced by fresh flowers overnight – is to be touched by the miracle of wild flowers and to hunger for the freedom and mystery of the countryside in which they normally grow.

GROWING WILD FLOWERS

There's more advice about setting up a wild flower 'conservation' garden about now. If I'd read some of it, about well-drained areas in full sun – and specific soil types, I'd never have started! Experiment – it's unlikely anything you do will be a total disaster! With wild flower gardens, there aren't any rigid procedures.

☐ My garden seems to have worked because I set out to recreate the wild flower mixture I saw up the clump. Peter and I made a note of the plants the butterflies landed on – and stayed on (birdsfoot-trefoil, valerian, scabious, herb robert) and we'd make sure these were the seeds we collected.

☐ If you start from scratch, as I did, you could use commercial seeds in your first year – and then collect from the wild. I ordered my earth in the late summer, so I could take advantage of the autumn seeding.

☐ I think it's best not to sow in neat rows. We sprinkled the seeds on the soil on a warm, damp day. You can do this either in the autumn as soon as you collect the seeds or in the spring after the frosts have stopped – late March and April. Don't cover them deeply; a fine sprinkling to 'anchor' them is enough. Seeds in the wild don't get sown in a neat row and covered with dirt!

☐ Can you find old wooden logs or tree-stumps? We saved the bases from our Christmas trees. These gently decayed and attracted insects and fungi!

☐ Some flowers – like foxgloves – are a two-year investment (biennial) but they are worth waiting for.

☐ Some flowers are best avoided until you feel expert as they are difficult to grow from seed and must never be uprooted from the wild: cowslips, wood anemones, primroses and bluebells.

☐ Don't over-garden and fiddle about. Let the plants grow large enough for you to identify them before you start any thinning and weeding. Some plants like hogweed and poppies may eventually need thinning out – but you'll soon discover which these are! Overall, wild plants are pretty adept at sorting themselves out!

☐ A buddleia bush is a wonderful long-term investment for a butterfly garden – in fact its other name is butterfly bush! These shrubs are widely available from garden centres. We were fortunate enough to have one growing on our dry-stone wall already.

☐ It does take a little time for anything to happen in the garden. Peter and I would pretend. We sat together looking at the bare earth and talking as though the flowers and butterflies were already there . . .
'Look at that blue butterfly – isn't he lovely?'
'Any second now, I bet he'll leave that clover and land on the trefoil . . . '
'Don't get too close, your shadow'll fall on him . . . '

Who wants to know what we've found?

Of course knowledge is valuable for its own sake but I think most of us would like to take the next step and use what we know. Sometimes that's a problem – especially for children.

The time came when we had been visiting the clump for a full year round and seen the dark purple sweet violets twice come and go. Our robin was still with us and we felt much more at home with wild plants and local birds. Trees we still found harder to identify (they continued to all look the same to me) – but after one special 'stolen' day, butterflies had become a new passion.

After the inevitable cold monotony of the early months of that year, one glorious March day could not be resisted. I had a day away from work and I asked Peter if he was doing anything important at school? Not, of course, that I expected an objective answer, but it was far too beautiful a day for any child to be indoors. We packed a picnic and went up the clump. So, too, did a large proportion of Bristol's office workers, looking as furtive as we did!

It was on that day that we saw our first huge, brilliant yellow brimstone butterfly. These winter as butterflies – they hibernate and emerge at the first warmth of the sun. Our brimstone followed a lazy, loose pattern in its flight – and we stalked it for most of the day. From then on we were hooked on butterflies! The clump also lured the elegant marbled white butterflies – black marbling on white – and these crowded round the tips of the long grass and the knapweed, flicking up and away at the slightest fall of our shadows.

Although we now know so much more about natural history, I still marvel at the wonders that were there for us to find, in a stretch of scrub a few yards from Bristol Zoo and the ice-cream vans. So close to the road. It dawned on us, of course, that our clump was such a modest patch – and that the miracles here must be duplicated in quantity and probably surpassed in quality as it were, in so many other areas. This was going on all around us. Did anyone else know about this?

We wanted to find a way to tell everyone – but at the same time feared for the safety of our clump. This is the naturalist's dilemma, longing to share but uneasily acknowledging the need to protect. And the fears are rarely without foundation. In our little clump alone, wood anemones have been uprooted and stolen, cropping has meant the total disappearance of some flowers and the determined shaving of the long grass by a Manpower Services Scheme has sent the marbled white butterflies packing.

But there *had* to be a safe way to share what we'd found – and Peter was finding the secrecy very restricting. Solving this problem for him took us one rung up the ladder into more adventures and deeper involvement. Quite simply, we got lucky!

In 1981, *The Times* started to publish a weekly Nature diary, the *Nature Notes*. This was a small column in the Information Section on the back page. Alongside the Art and Music notices, the Nature Diarist, known mysteriously only as DJM announced the equally important countryside exhibitions of cow parsley, willowherb and lime blossom – and alerted us to the current stars of bird-song. Much of what we saw on Sunday up the clump, DJM would tell his readers to look out for in his column on Monday morning – and this coincidence seemed to us remarkable. We pretended to search for DJM, telling each other he must be hiding up a tree listening for our observations!

We agreed that as we were already sharing with the Diarist in spirit, it might be an idea to ask him if he would like us to share with him in fact. So I wrote to DJM at *The Times*, telling him how much we enjoyed his *Nature Notes* – and how we found them uncannily true to our own experience. I described our activities and asked DJM if he would be interested in hearing our localised West Country observations.

It's quite a boost just to find the cheek to do these things and I don't think we expected a reply at all. We were thrilled to receive an encouraging letter by return. DJM replied that he would be most interested in what we saw. Peter immediately requested the job of observer/correspondent (I'd hoped he would, of course) and now gained for himself the most important reason of all for looking hard, identifying correctly – and making records: someone 'official' wanted to know.

This became Peter's first adult correspondence apart from family letters – and our first contact with the spectacular generosity of adults towards children who share their interests, children they will probably never meet. For the next few months, Nature reporting was a very sober affair and to start with, Peter took over all the actual field recording (a pain in the neck in wet and windy weather). He then wrote a long account every week or ten days, each account dated and with a note of the location. These letters took him up to two hours.

At nine years old, Peter found this a lot of writing at one go, especially as much of the vocabulary was specialised – bird and flower names. I suggested that he just write one or two paragraphs each evening – but Peter pointed out that by the time he was finished, the report would be out of date. True. So he simply learned the spellings and got on with it. In return for which I didn't nag so much about his untidy bedroom and took back a lot of routine jobs he'd been doing. It was a question of priorities.

Monday mornings, *Nature Notes* days, were immensely exciting – because some Mondays brought Peter's observations incorporated into DJM's tersely descriptive prose and usually prefaced by 'In the West Country . . . '

All discoveries were duly reported and sometimes Peter sent a 'spring update' announcing a single item – 'The violet buds have opened!' We were normally seeing the more commonplace plants and birds but, as the Avon Gorge is host to an enchanting variety of plants we did start to find rarities. (We noticed, though, that textbooks differ on what is widespread and what is rare!) Early spring cinquefoil was our first truly rare discovery. This is a tiny, five-petalled flower of a defiantly vivid yellow, flowering in March in the open, rocky grassland around the clump. When we first saw a patch of spring cinquefoil, breathtakingly bright as we emerged, blinking from the darker woodland, we were spellbound and Peter rushed home to look up what he had seen and to write to DJM. The Diarist was most encouraging: 'How lucky you are to find the spring cinquefoil!' We were, by coincidence, on a clump visit to listen for the chiff-chaff as DJM had instructed Peter to do.

Sometimes we photocopied Peter's reports before posting them – because Peter had started to run a Nature Magazine and the reports could be used in articles. Peter's report for September 1982 reads:

Nature Report
9th September 1982
Avon Gorge Woods

The bright yellow flowers of tansy line in ranks along the paths. Bees and

27

butterflies cram around sheep's-bit getting drowsy on the nectar in the stamens. The beautiful fluted buds of harebells rest near to their 'parents' – the fully opened flower. Rubbery fungus collects on the fallen-off branches of oak trees. As you walk into the oak woods, you are likely to hear immature nuthatches 'practising' cracking nuts on oak trees: a skill which their name comes from.

Beechnut cases lie on woodland paths like little brown four-pointed stars. The lovely blue flowers of milkwort almost shelter under the bigger plants of birdsfoot trefoil. Conkers fall like hard wooden balls onto the ground. Fallen leaves circle the trees they fell from.

Craneflies blunder in the grass, their long legs waving wildly about. The long shoots of bramble hang down from trees like party streamers. Tiny tormentil flowers are still in profusion under the protection of the oak tree.

11th September 1982

Piles of downy feathers remain from when the young birds pull their 'fluff' out. What was the young sparrow broods are now very much similar to their parents. As well as the berries, hawthorn leaves turn red. Red admirals crowd on ivy flowers. Pignut's delicate flowers are still in bloom. Silk button spangle gall is alongside ordinary spangle gall on oak leaves.

A report sent in January 1984 reveals the need to look beyond looking – and a certain desperation!

Nature Report
6th January 1984
Bristol Downs and Ashton Court Estate

The apple-green leaves of alexanders are growing and spreading out. They have reached about 18 inches high. Moss shows very green on the bark of dead – and sometimes alive trees. Carpets of goosegrass cover the ground under the hawthorns. The seed leaves of this plant are very interesting – like most cotyledons. The seed leaves are totally different from the normal leaf. In this case, they are a pair of fat, privet-like leaves.

Sycamore keys hang down in large bunches. A surprising and alarming number of midges and gnats are around this year. Most of the berries from the holly bushes have been stolen by the birds and this has robbed the area of colour.

The white fluff of old man's beard is still around, clinging to the bushes like left-over Christmas decorations. Looking up at the branches of oak trees, there is an abnormal amount of oak apples: as many as six may be on the end of a branch.

Violet buds are still tightly packed. WHEN WILL THEY OPEN? Wood pigeons feed on ivy berries. They fly off in large clumps when approached. The leaves of green hellebore are coming through under a sweet chestnut tree.

Nature reporting for DJM has continued every week or so since 1982. Keith made Peter a badge with NATURE REPORTER on it – and Peter wore this on his camouflage jacket to give him confidence (especially if we took our reporting to Kent and were creeping under barbed wire into the game preserves).

In 1983, an appealingly illustrated selection of the *Nature Notes* entries for 1981–2 was published (*The Times Nature Diary* by Derwent May, illustrated by Richard Blake, Robson Books). Mr May sent Peter an inscribed copy on publication day. Knowing since the previous December that the book was to be published, and eagerly waiting for it to come out since then, Peter was shaking too much with excitement to open it himself! Derwent May, we learned from the cover of the book, is a novelist and literary editor of the *Listener*. It's fantastic to feel that you *matter* to the wider world – that you've got knowledge to offer – especially at nine years old! This, I think, is how the whimsical, loyal (it's still going on) letter friendship between Peter and the literary editor of the *Listener* gave him the courage to reach out to other experts in Nature study – and put us all firmly on the winding path towards the extraordinary adventures to come . . .

Just one success fortifies children through literally dozens of charming brush-offs. And written to children, they will be charming. It's unlikely – I would go so far as to say impossible – that the media would be as arbitrary in their rejection of offers of 'help' from children as yes, I know they can be to adults.

Peter now sent off letters left, right and centre. Back came acknowledgements – and refusals which were in themselves informative and kindly. *The Times* is unfailingly courteous and gentle – and we always know their replies on the doormat by their ancient typefaces! When his *Nature Notes* editor, Derwent May, wrote to the correspondence page of *The Times* about the 'ornithological anachronism' in the use of the bird-song of the collared dove in films set in Britain before 1955, Peter promptly wrote to the paper describing the popularity of the willow-warbler's song with television producers. *The Times* replied by return:

Dear Peter,
    The Editor asks me to thank you for your most interesting and well-written letter. Although he was not able to publish it, he asks me to say that he is most impressed by your skill in identifying bird-song.

Blue Peter were kindly and encouraging (Peter wrote to them about giant hogweed) and Peter's frequent correspondence with the youth division of the *Royal Society for the Protection of Birds* was full of lively information. Prized, though with mixed feelings, is a long letter from Peter Holden (Youth Organiser of the RSPB and a respected bird authority) asking Peter if he was *sure* he actually saw the rare firecrest – or perhaps, *surely* it was the more common goldcrest? (It *was* a firecrest, I was there.)

One of our local radio stations was the curtest in its written response, simply informing Peter that they couldn't give him any insight into their Nature coverage because they didn't do any. However, you can't win them all – and I think proper research on our part could have prevented this. A few years later, though, to anticipate for a second, Peter was to give a talk on local radio all about badgers – and was to be treated as consultant by the station which in these early days had no Nature coverage . . .

WRITING LETTERS

Wouldn't it be wonderful if experts in every field of human endeavour wrote regularly to children who wanted to make this kind of friendship! And, if our experience holds true for others, more experts are willing to do this than we realise. The potential is enormous.

☐ Who to write to? A good place to start is the letter pages of magazines aimed at children – in Peter's case this was *Bird Life*, the RSPB magazine of the Youth Ornithologists' Club. Peter sent letters and poems to the special readers' pages. None were published, but all were fully and appreciatively acknowledged. The pleasure for Peter seemed to come from the letters – he didn't seem to mind if what he sent was published or not. Peter took part in the bird surveys and competitions and this helped the joining-in habit. Eventually he had the courage to write to papers and magazines about what interested *him*. It definitely takes more cheek to write an unsolicited letter and I think you have to wait until the time 'feels' right. In our case, this was when we were bursting with information and longing to put it to use.

☐ I explained to Peter that it was polite (and effective) to show a detailed interest in what the paper or magazine had to say and to explain exactly how the paper had inspired him to write. This sounds complicated, but it's as simple as:

Dear Bird Life,

I loved your article about goldcrests on page 6 of this month's issue. I didn't know they were smaller than wrens. We have some in a bush at the end of our road – which is amazing as it's so close to a main road with lots of lorries.

We have been looking hard at goldcrests after your article and yesterday, in the woods on the side of the Avon Gorge, I saw a firecrest! It was against the sun and its scarlet crest was sticking up. It was singing to a female and didn't notice us so we watched it for a long time. I believe firecrests are rare.

☐ There are many practical ways we can make letter writing easier for our children. To start with, when Peter was 8, I gave him encouragement and practical help for every letter he wanted to write, sitting with him, assuring him that what he wanted to say was just fine – and giving him the letter layout if he needed reminding. Here is a specimen letter – and as this was not a personal letter, I've included the recipient's address, in the manner of a business letter:

23 Hollygate Road
Bristol BS6 8TK
5th March 1982

Blue Peter
BBC TV
Wood Lane
London W12 7RJ

Dear Blue Peter,

I was very interested in today's news about peculiar bird behaviour – especially the friendly robin. Our peculiar bird is a blackbird. This blackbird lives in our road and he starts to sing in the middle of the night every time our bathroom light gets put on.

Yours sincerely,

PETER TAYLOR (aged 10)

I would also usually write the envelope for Peter. I notice from the letters I receive that a lot of mothers do this for their children. Perhaps the envelope is the last straw – or we are anxious to make sure it is accurate and does get to its destination after all the effort!

☐ Peter's 13 now and my job is to provide paper, an empty table, a long undisturbed time, an appreciative audience – and the inevitable cup of tea.

☐ Sometimes it's hard *not* to prompt or to correct spellings but in this kind of correspondence, it's vital to avoid taking over. Children's turn of phrase is inimitable and genuine – and this letter isn't going to be marked or graded. It's not for school. Anyway, if you dictate, it won't sound right – and, frankly, the recipient will rumble you.

☐ It *is* important to signify that the letter is from a child as it isn't always possible to deduce this from the handwriting. A signature like Peter Taylor (aged 10) will encourage a softer response! Peter objects to putting his age now – so he doesn't; but it opened many, many doors for him in the past.

☐ It's standard procedure to send a stamped addressed envelope if you are asking for information. I'd advise sending one anyway.

Part two
IN TOUCH

Running a magazine: the launch!

Small acts of kindness from adults live on in children's memories – sometimes with consequences reaching down the generations. Heirlooms of the spirit.

When I was 9 and at primary school, my best friend and I had wanted to run a magazine. Lots of children do – and the first issue, while entertaining, is usually the last. Production is the stumbling block. My friend's father offered to type, carbon and staple 10 copies of each magazine for us, no easy task for a non-typist who had, I suspect, to fit this into his lunch hour at work. He was also, as I found out later, a man whose family circumstances were beset with anxiety and tragedy.

With the publicity and support given to us by our school headmaster, our own magazine of stories and news events ran every fortnight for a year. Then my friend's mother was arrested for shoplifting and the local paper was brutal in its front-page coverage of the offence and its implication that this had been going on for a long time . . . The shame was too much for the family to bear. Nowadays I hope there would be more understanding – the woman was obviously ill and desperately unhappy. They moved house, quite abruptly, and I was heartbroken to lose my friend. The memory of her father's reliable generosity remains – he so badly wanted a happy family; I could sense this even as a child. I'm glad that Peter's enthusiasm for a similar magazine venture gives me the chance to pass on the kindness I learned by his example.

Soon after I told him the story of our primary school magazine Peter wanted to start a magazine about Nature. This is such an enormous subject, of course, that he sensibly decided to limit the contents to what was happening locally to the plants, birds, trees, insects – and furry life when we were lucky enough to see it!

I type (which is handy but not essential as some children prefer hand-written work), and Keith is interested in graphics and printing – so we offered to help with the technicalities of production as long as Peter provided the writing and the drawings. We would all think about publicity and distribution when we had the magazine. And in view of the major setback to come, it's a good thing we did plan it this way, simply assuming that there would be hordes of eager buyers.

The right title for a magazine is vital. I held back any suggestions, knowing that Peter must find his own title. Production was delayed while Peter mulled over his list: *Eagle Eye, Eagle Eye on Nature, Eyes Around Us, Eagle Eye on Nature*. Finally, he put them together, dropped the eagle and came up with the lovely *Eye on Local Nature*. Peter then explained that he would rather run a magazine with a friend – like I had done – than do it alone. Fortunately his best friend Matt agreed and could bring to the magazine a keen interest in seashore life as well as regular frog reports from the well-stocked pond in his garden.

This, then, is the story of *Eye on Local Nature*, the magazine launched in April 1982 by two 9-year old primary school boys. Not that there's anything unusual in the beginning of the venture. It's what it led to in the years that followed that's remarkable.

Back to the beginning of the story! Peter and Matt spent an afternoon in Peter's room, giggling and experimenting with the design for the front cover. Matt is an expert in three-dimensional writing and was therefore in charge of designing the lettering for the title. The boys decided that there should be eight pages and the price should be 12p.

The boys wrote their articles and passed them to me. I unobtrusively corrected the spelling – resisting all temptation to rephrase – and typed out the articles for them. The magazine was to be A5 size and Keith had devised a means of printing it (see Appendix One). I usually left space somewhere on the page for an illustration to be done afterwards in black biro (drawing ink came later). The boys told me where they wanted their picture to go and I drew a blue line around the area so I would avoid typing in it. I used a pale blue crayon because most photocopy machines do not 'pick up' pale blue. Matt and Peter decided which article would go where, the middle pages carrying the star feature. All completed, I gave the sheets to Keith for his part of the production. When the pages had been assembled and photocopied, Keith folded them and stapled the magazine in the middle, ready for distribution.

Now a collector's item, the first issue of *Eye on Local Nature* contained one of Peter's mazes with a Nature bias – help the bee to get to its hive – and the first of a continuing series of pond reports by Matt:

POND NEWS

by Matt Jones

In ponds the tadpoles will now have come
out of their jelly and will have grown quite
a lot. In the pond at our house, there is
a large amount of leeches but this has not
affected the amount of tadpoles in our pond,
and, in fact I have not seen a single tadpole
with a leech sticking on to it.

Most of the plants around our pond
(reeds, liverworts etc) are now showing new
shoots. This year the frogs actually layed
some spawn, we were glad of this because it
was the first time they had layed any spawn
whatsoever in our pond.

12th April 1982

Peter wrote his Bristol Nature Report:

BRISTOL NATURE REPORT

by Peter Taylor

Reporting from the Avon Gorge, and Ashton
Court areas

On rocks in a very sunny glade the flowers
of the rare spring cinquefoil are evident, their
lovely yellow flowers reflecting the sun's rays.
Bullfinches (with their beautiful breasts),
male and female are bathing in muddy puddles,
(the female is smaller and has a duller breast
than the male). Squirrels are very active;
while blue-tits, robins and blackbirds are

lively, flying from branch to branch and singing. Mouse-ear chickweed is flowering, and so
is valerian, coming into flower on exposed
rocks overlooking the river Avon.

  Cowslips are coming out among the brambles
and grass, looking remarkably like daffodils!
Wood anemones are out in full flower, their
leaves penetrating even the thickest blankets
of dead leaves. While most of the violets
(dog and sweet)die, the late wood violets come
up. Near to the wood violets is buxbaums -
or Persian speedwell; however, the less evident
wood speedwell is coming up more slowly.

  The drumming of the greater-spotted
woodpeckers is evident. Tree-creepers
climb trees from one end to another.

  Long-tailed tits collect feathers to
line their nests.

        12th April 1982

This was followed by two pages of appeal to readers to contribute articles, ideas and pictures. The cover of the magazine was pretty rudimentary:

At the end of the magazine the boys drew their trademark – deciding to call themselves *Harvest Mouse and Oak Productions*. Matt was the oak and Peter the harvest mouse. This gave the enterprise an official feel!

Keith undertook the photocopying of 20 launch copies and the boys went off to school keen to spread the word and to sell them . . .

But distribution met a painful setback. The children's headmaster refused to let Matt and Peter approach parents and other children in the playground after school to sell copies. Or even to sell any copies at school. He explained to me that this could lead to some sort of protection racket as was taking place on the coaches at a local secondary school. I was dumbfounded; a less likely couple of racketeers than Peter and Matt it was hard to imagine. But there's really no arguing with that kind of reaction.

The refusal was a double blow because the boys' early surge of enthusiasm would have given them the courage to make the approach to parents and other children. And they did want to involve their classmates in the magazine.

To be fair, the headmaster kindly presented the boys with a prize for their efforts in producing the first copy – but this was missing the point. Peter and Matt wanted to be taken seriously as Editors of a magazine which would grow in circulation. This launch issue wasn't to be the beginning and end of it all.

It was up to us to step in and help the children with distribution. I encouraged Peter to approach neighbours and local shopkeepers. He found this embarrassing after the disappointment of the school refusal – and galling to receive pleasant enquiries about how many of his classmates and teachers were buying copies. Peter profusely apologised to each potential purchaser for the sheer imposition of what he was trying to sell. All the adults were very kind – many paid him more than 12p, telling him to put the extra towards production costs – and the first issue sold so well that more had to be printed!

Times change of course. Peter and Matt are just about to go back to their old primary school to spend an afternoon advising on the school's conservation garden. The new headmistress is proud of the boys and their link with the school. It all depends on individuals. Perhaps if the headmaster had encouraged the magazine within the school, we wouldn't have had to look outside it – and that would have been to miss far, far more!

The little magazine grew – and the story of how it grew, and who helped and befriended the children is an inspiration in what for many of us seem harsh and worrying times. In the next three years, *Eye on Local Nature* was to attract not only the children it set out to involve, but experts in all fields of conservation, school inspectors, television and radio producers, *Times* journalists, artists, photographers, pensioners, housewives, teachers – and numerous university dons.

How *Eye on Local Nature* grew

At the same time that Issue One was selling out, Peter and Matt were working on Issue Two. In the beginning, the magazine appeared every fortnight but three months of this taught us that the pace was too fast for all of us – including purchasers! We soon agreed on one issue each month – and this gave us time for discussion, planning and above all, relishing of each issue.

The mainstay of *Eye on Local Nature* was always articles by the two boys but the idea was to involve other children. However, the magazine was more or less banned from the school – and so adults rallied to help. The school secretary gave the children a delightful piece about swifts:

> <u>THE SWIFTS ARE BACK</u> – by Alix Lord
>
> The swifts are back. Every May these sooty, fast flying birds with their thin crescent wings return to nest in Britain from their African winter home.
>
> This year they were seen over Leigh Woods on May 3 and the next day they were screaming round Bristol houses. In the next few weeks they will nest under the eves of houses. They feed on insects and only land to lay eggs and feed the young; they even sleep on the wing!
>
> They will leave for Africa sometime in August.

Adults proved themselves well able to adapt to the unselfconscious spirit of the magazine – and, we discovered, liked being published. However, an adult contribution for the third issue brought the first real editorial problem for the children. Peter had made friends with John Mowat, a retired lecturer from a local college of education, merely by passing his door every day on the way to school and saying hallo. John was an obvious person to approach to buy the magazine – and Peter was dismayed when his article should be the one to cause problems. John's article contained Latin names: he had written out the Latin for each flower he described. Latin names, Peter decided (not having yet come to terms with them himself) would frighten people off – especially children. Peter seemed to regard them as almost indecent. Peter found himself juggling with the demands of friendship and the likely frightening effect of too much scholarship on any children who might be persuaded to read his magazine. He decided to leave the Latin out.

Fortunately, John didn't appear to be in the least offended. He continued to give us regular articles about local wildlife – with Latin – and we continued to publish them every month without Latin. As the boys grew more familiar with botany, however, they began to see that the Latin classifications served some purpose other than to frighten – and once we had all read about the amazing life of Linnaeus (upon whose system our plant classifications are based), Latin crept in more comfortably.

Peter and Matt were able to make their own decision on this early problem. A little later on, though, I had to step in to decide what to do about a local, very talented lady who bombarded us with articles and narrative sagas of a metaphysical nature – elephants jumping over the Universe, meditating ants – that kind of thing. Some of her poems would have occupied whole issues – but she meant well. I edited her offerings to their more factual basis and left out the elephants on the grounds that it wasn't actually local Nature.

When we planned the third issue of the magazine, we had one page unaccounted for. Peter rejected the idea of another maze, or more Nature jokes. Instead, he asked me to write something, so that I would be joining in *properly*, not just doing the typing. I knew exactly what he meant but I didn't know what to write. What about a story? We agreed that this might encourage children to join in. It was May and I had just been reading about the diabolical habits of cuckoos. These habits are so amazing that I thought I could combine a little fact with a lot of fiction and produce something amusing. Self-consciously directing it towards 'younger readers', I wrote an episode and read it to Matt and Peter who were gratifyingly (or politely – you can never quite tell when children are humouring you!) pleased and offered to provide the pictures for it. And so *The Great Cuckoo Problem* began. Once I got started, I found it was exciting to write a story in which something dramatic happens in a small number of words – with a compulsory cliff-hanger at the end. I've always admired the skill in compression of strip-cartoonists who do this all the time – remember *Rupert?* I had no idea what was going to happen past the cliff-hanger because I made up the story issue by issue, usually at the last moment and cutting down the words as I typed it out and could see the space on the page running out. The story lasted for ten episodes and broke the ice for others to write for us in ways we had not anticipated. A correspondence page began . . .

CORRESPONDENCE PAGE

Emma Emms writes to the Editors:

My 'great cuckoo problem' is – I have just spent two weeks in a remote part of Cornwall and one weekend in the heart of Devon – I was listening and waiting all the time to hear the cuckoo – but no. Please tell me if you have heard him and if so where. I have missed it now for several years.

I am glad to report that we saw lots of butterflies but all browns of some sort or other – no common blue. I am wondering where you were photographing these blues (Issue 5) ? I haven't seen them for years!

Peter replies

I have not heard any cuckoos either, but I think I have seen one in Nightingale Valley. My publisher reports that they are alive and noisy in Chew Magna.

You will also find, Emma, that there are lots of common blues in the sunny parts of Ashton Court – near to the Mansion and the woods. I will draw you a map upon request. Thank you for your letter.

The magazine's first celebrity article was sent by Peter Holden, National Organiser of the Young Ornithologists' Club, the junior section of the Royal Society for the Protection of Birds. Peter threw the article about in the air with whoops of glee! Here at last was a big name! Fame! The article accompanied a letter to Peter about firecrests in reply to Peter's reported sighting of one in the Avon Gorge Woods. Firecrests are minute, delicate and noisy birds, rare in Britain and related to the more common goldcrest. Goldcrests and firecrests are the tiniest birds in Europe – and enchantingly colourful and active. Firecrests have a whitish eyestripe and a brilliant red mohican tuft.

When Peter and I saw the firecrest, we clung together shaking with excitement and wonder: the tuft was raised high and shimmering, backlit by the sun. Peter wrote at once to Mr Holden to report the sighting and sent him a copy of *Eye on Local Nature*. Mr Holden replied by return, congratulating Peter on his magazine, enclosing an article for it – but questioning the firecrest sighting. Was Peter *sure* it was a firecrest? Peter had not mentioned the white eyestripe and, as Mr Holden reminded him, 'Male goldcrests do, of course, also have darker yellow centres to their crown.'

Peter's dismay at the questioning of his sighting was amply compensated for by the celebrity article. And interestingly, we were later to discover that firecrests *had* been recorded in the area where we saw them – but that there was some feeling among the birdwatchers concerned that it was better to keep quiet about this. Mr Holden, though, wrote about his favourite birds with an encouraging simplicity just right for the magazine.

There is a form of approval – a 'rubber-stamping' of a venture which, simply because it does not come from naturally biased family and friends can only come from people who are successful experts in their field. And if one celebrity praised the magazine, this could be shown to another celebrity and the whole business of 'trading up' could begin!

The boys decided to increase the number of copies of the magazine in which Peter Holden's article appeared so that magazines could be sent to other experts who could then see that Mr Holden had endorsed *Eye on Local Nature*. This set the formula for the magazine's future: articles and drawings by the Editors, articles by local adults, occasional celebrity articles – and tireless pleas for children to join in.

But why couldn't *Eye on Local Nature* reach the children for whom it was originally launched? Although Peter and Matt pleaded for articles in their Editorials, no children were writing for it. This worried us far more than it needed to – and frustrated us at times. One little boy who came across the magazine made two long phone calls to us about the article on butterflies he was writing for the boys – and despite all our encouragement, the article never came. What emerged was what I'm sure every teacher knows. Children love the idea of writing an article or sending in a drawing and they will usually start one. At this point, though, they need a lot of encouragement to complete it. I think, too, there needs to be the right time and the right environment.

I'd always been dubious of school teaching time set aside for children to write an 'inspired' article for the school magazine, but now I was beginning to have a lot more sympathy for the idea – and wondering how to apply it. We had to get children's articles before the two boys became despondent about this – and, frankly, before the magazine became too adult. Five months after the launch of the magazine our first child article appeared. This was not a direct result of the boys' pleas for articles. I suppose it might seem like 'cheating' – but it was a piece of writing I 'commissioned' from a child I was teaching.

I taught Antony and Peter (both 9) together for 'lessons' in the summer holidays. This sounds stern, but it was a lot of fun, Antony's best friend also requesting to come to a 'teacher' for morning lessons! One of my lessons was a close observation and natural camouflage session up the clump. It tipped with rain, Bristol fashion, but we went anyway, despite Antony's loud reservations. Intricate observation was tricky under the circumstances – so I desperately thought up an idea to discuss on the spot and to use for written work on our return home. Antony wrote his advice on how to keep cheerful on long country walks in Britain when it is pouring with rain!

Operation Newshound

With eight issues of *Eye on Local Nature* under their belts, Peter and Matt decided it was time to stop waiting for articles to come to them – and to go out in search of news! Operation Newshound was born in September 1982, followed by Operation Ferret and Operation Scoop!

Where better to start than the local zoo – which, I should imagine, is well used to similar requests from children. Peter and Matt wrote to the Director of Bristol Zoo who replied in charming terms:

> Dear Peter,
> Thank you very much for your letter and the copies of your excellent magazine for local young naturalists. I am sure one of our keepers would be delighted to be interviewed by you and Matt Jones . . .

The two boys prepared thoroughly for this interview. Matt's mother took them round the zoo to refresh their memories of what was there and to inspire relevant questions. Matt and Peter worked out for themselves that to get interesting answers, they needed interesting questions. They prepared six questions each and wrote them out on a sheet of paper attached to a clipboard, leaving several lines blank underneath each question to jot down the reply.

The two ten-year old newshounds wanted to conduct this interview on their own, without any adults hovering around. We agreed and arranged a time with the zoo over the telephone. The boys took the Director's letter as their admission ticket – and left home an hour too early, clutching their clipboards and rehearsing loudly!

Several hours later, Matt and Peter returned – thrilled to bits by the time they had had – and falling over themselves to tell us about it and show us the reptile skins that they had been given as souvenirs. Reptile skins smell like old socks and Peter still has his pinned to his bedroom pinboard!

The zoo interview was the star feature of Issue 9 and copies were sent, along with the important 'thank you' to the zoo Director and to the keeper who had given the interview and taken the boys behind the scenes.

Operation Ferret, Peter's personal ambition to interview BBC Natural History prize-winning producer Caroline Weaver, needed both the courage to make the request – and the tenacity implied in the campaign's name. It's hard to catch Miss Weaver in this country. She is the producer of *Badger Watch* and the hard-hitting *Greenpeace: Commandos of Conservation*, and is much in demand. But when she is not abroad filming, Caroline Weaver lives nearby. Peter passed her house on his way to school – and his retired lecturer friend had introduced them. When Peter finally caught her at home and asked her to give him an interview, Miss Weaver agreed at once. She asked Peter to come round straight away! Peter grabbed his clipboard, wrote down five questions and rushed off in his usual state of agitation.

As well as a kindly, relaxed interview (it's obvious from the neat, full answers Peter was able to write on his questionnaire that Miss Weaver sympathetically allowed him lots of time), Peter has magic memories of her welcome, her tea – and her chocolate cake.

Caroline Weaver became a regular subscriber – and writer for the magazine – and Peter was particularly proud of this friendship.

So far, interviews were turning out to be pleasant experiences, not as daunting once they had started as the boys had supposed. Operation Newshound and Operation Ferret had succeeded. Operation Scoop was yet to come . . .

BEGINNING TO INTERVIEW

This is a big step for children to take. For a short time, they will be crossing over into the adult world, becoming initiators and investigators.

☐ Adult experts respond well to polite written requests for a small – and specified – amount of their time. Peter usually asked for half-an-hour and the two boys were usually rewarded with two or three hours – once a whole day!

☐ Always enclose a stamped addressed envelope with the interview request. I used to write these for Peter.

☐ If there is time, preparation is a guarantee of success. Thinking about relevant questions is best – then deciding on up to 6, writing these out neatly and leaving room for an answer and extra information as well.

☐ If the request for interview is made over the telephone, you may have to act quickly. Some experts have said to Peter, 'Come round *now* . . . ' This kind of invitation has to be met at once with equal enthusiasm! This means it's best to have some ideas ready in advance of the request.

☐ A clipboard to rest on and to stop the paper flapping about is essential – and so are extra biros and pencils.

☐ If the interview is to be conducted out of doors – as most of the boys' interviews were – it's best to discuss what will happen if the weather is dreadful. We usually made an agreement to go anyway and I feel the experts respected the children for this.

☐ The boys always followed up the interview with a thank you letter and a copy of the magazine in which the interview appeared.

The local paper

How, I wondered enviously as a child, did our Kent local paper actually hear of the accomplishments and ambitions of other local children? Why didn't it ever show any interest in mine? Did reporters rove around, discovering children? How could I attract their attention?

I was shocked and disillusioned beyond measure when I learned that parents sent in news items about their own children! This was boasting far beyond my youthful comprehension. Now I know it's the way of the world. The magazine readers kept asking us when the local paper was going to discover what was going on – and write about the children.

We held an *Eye-on* conference and decided that if, by seeking publicity in the local paper, more children might be involved, and more magazines circulated around Bristol, then it would be worthwhile. We didn't know how to go about getting this publicity and therefore chose a rather oblique, modest approach.

Full of hope, Peter and Matt wrote about *Eye on Local Nature* to the Editor of the *Bristol Evening Post*, sending him copies of the magazine and asking him to tell them his favourite place for Nature. The Editor's reply was to the point: 'In answer to your question, my favourite wildlife place in Bristol is Blaise Castle.'

That's the end of that then, we thought. The boys aren't going to be discovered this month. Perhaps our approach was a little *too* modest and sideways. However, surprisingly, a reporter from the paper telephoned a few days later asking for an interview with the boys. Matt and Peter prepared themselves for this with back copies of the magazine to give away, and a determination to interview the reporter about *his* favourite place for Nature.

Over the telephone, the reporter had given me a firm lecture about wanting to see the boys on his own. So, when the young man came to our flat, I gave him a tray of tea and shut the door on them all.

In little less time than it took to drink the tea, the interview was over. Peter and Matt felt they hadn't given good answers to the reporter's questions about why they cared about Nature and why they ran the magazine. But they had managed to ask *him* a couple of questions – the reporter's favourite Nature place and bird were later incorporated into a magazine article.

There was then a very long silence. Many issues of the paper came and went. Had the article been dropped? We didn't seem to be having much luck in this campaign. We stopped eagerly looking through the local paper every evening – and forgot about the interview.

It came as a shock to the two boys when an *Evening Post* reporter appeared at the school one afternoon, weeks later. The two boys were instructed to collect the most impressive Nature books from the school library and go to the headmaster's study to be photographed. And the article and picture were printed the following day!

Now came an unexpected bonus in the campaign to reach more children. Following the favourable and attractive newspaper publicity – which reflected well on the children's school – the headmaster immediately took a great interest in the magazine and exhorted articles at morning assembly!

And now, at long last, a classmate produced an article. This was a special article because it showed us a maturity and tenderness in the two boys which I had never fully noticed. Matt procured a promised article about fish from a classmate who was not especially at ease with expressing himself on paper. The article is precious to us for 10-year old Graham's obvious love of his fish named Nero – and also for the care and dedication shown by the two Editors in helping me read the unusual hand-writing of the original and for Matt's faithful re-drawing of the fish so that it was in black ink suitable for photocopying. Graham's Fish was rapidly followed by an article on his Nature Club by 9-year old Martin:

OUR NATURE CLUB, by Martin Rogers of Redland

I go to a Nature Club and there are three others in it: John, Paul and Charlie. I have given them a Hawk Moth and a demolished Red Admiral. In the Club's collection we have a rhinoceros tooth and horn, a snake's skull and a stag beetle.

I have drawn the rhino horn.

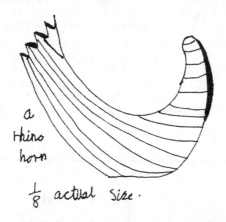

a rhino horn

⅛ actual size.

Boosted by a local paper story to refer to, the magazine's early difficulties in encouraging children to write began to disappear. In the years following, children were to send touchingly frank observations on what fascinates them in the world around us: how to keep snails as pets and whether they all coil in the same direction; dissecting owl pellets; collecting poppy seeds; what grows on tree-stumps; compost heaps; rockpools; pet rabbits returning to the wild; the habits of moles; robins; woodlice; the difference between frog and toad tadpoles; spindle trees and their peculiar berries; fungus; maybugs, and pasque flowers. The article on pasque flowers was sent to the magazine by its youngest contributor – 7-year old Jennifer Veale of Royston – a prizewinner in *The Times* 1984 Hedgewatch Competition – who responded to Peter's request for an article:

SPRING IN ROYSTON by Jennifer Veale

A Pasque
Flower J.V.

There is a heath near Royston
where Pasque flowers grow. I
walk through beech woods where
it is dark to a grassy hump.
The hump is made of chalk; it is
dry and very sunny. Pasque means
Easter in French and at Easter
lots of Pasque flowers grow.
They are growing on the side of
the hump where it is sunny.
There are cowslips too, but they
grow all over the hump.

The Pasque flowers have purple petals,
lots of bright yellow pollen and the
bees like the pollen very much.
All the plants are covered in little
hairs. When lots of flowers are
growing they look very beautiful, especially as they
are rare.

GETTING NOTICED

Publicity for children's achievements does matter – it gives them confidence and adds a certain status to their endeavour. So it's worth establishing good relationships with your local paper.

☐ It's essential to actually take the local paper for at least two weeks in advance if you intend to approach the reporters for coverage. Note down the kind of articles the named journalists write. Some are more sensational than others – liking human conflict and drama. I think these writers are best avoided. Track down the more serious reporters.

☐ Simply write to the journalist you choose c/o the local paper and tell him or her the main details of your story. I've found that journalists like lots of detail to work their stories from, but it's better to keep to one side of A4 paper, otherwise it looks obsessive. It's good if the children's school is involved in some way – there's certainly a higher chance of a photograph if it is.

☐ If there is no response after three or four days, telephone (*find* the courage) and ask for the journalist, saying you have telephoned to enquire if he or she is interested in the story – and are any more details needed? Even better if you can mention a new development.

☐ Persist. Try again another time. It's worth it. The rather reticent young man who came to our flat to interview Peter and Matt several years ago now has an excellent rapport with children. He's just taken a photographer to cover the story of Peter and Matt returning to their old primary school to give a talk on conservation and advise on the setting up of a wild flower garden and pond. He's also asked us to go through our archives – and could we send him the issue of the magazine which talked about *his* favourite bird and place for Nature? (back numbers of the magazine are much in demand these days!). And, happily, he's asked me to keep the local paper in touch with all future developments. This is good, because it's always easier to contact the local paper at their instigation.

Christmas magic

By Christmas 1982, we had far too many articles and drawings for one 8-page issue. We'd also made a rule to include all or part of every article sent – especially from a child or a new contributor. We didn't want to keep any writer waiting for more than a month to see his or her work in print. This had proved to be the way to entice contributors to write again. Keith suggested that the Christmas issue be 12 pages, even though this would take much longer to type, collate and staple – and would cost us more. But we decided it was to be our Christmas present to our readers, our Christmas bonus issue.

The Christmas *Eye on Local Nature* was a fair old mixture! It contained nostalgia – some of Matt's jokes, one of Peter's mazes – and this seemed the right time to reproduce the photograph of the two boys from the local newspaper. The two main features, though, were new. Variety matters. We included an invitation to join us on a Boxing Day Nature Walk in Leigh Woods – with a map of the route – and an interview with master wood carver, RSPB Warden, John Waldon.

Our 'discovery' of John Waldon has about it the magic just right for Christmas warmth. Like all 'discoveries', it came in a roundabout way. The previous Christmas, we had been developing our interest in up-the-clump birdwatching – and Keith found small wooden bird brooches for sale on our Christmas visit to the Bristol Museum. They were priced £3.50 – cheap for such intricate carving. Keith bought me a robin to commemorate our clump friend. Behind the brooch was a card mount with a label giving Mr Waldon's address.

I loved that brooch so much that Keith encouraged me to write to Mr Waldon to ask him what other birds he carved. Eventually I wrote – and back came an amazingly exhaustive list and an offer to carve anything I especially wanted not among his 'current brood'.

So, for a year after this, I celebrated each new bird we identified by ordering the bird of the month! Some were birds Mr Waldon did not stock – and had not carved before – and I gather he had a lot of difficulty carving the intricate beak of the treecreeper I requested! Once I 'cheated' and ordered a nuthatch because I loved the colourful, pink and blue illustrations of them in our bird book. However, guilt at cheating fuelled my determination to locate nuthatches – and we succeeded the following month. Nuthatches are all over the place in Leigh Woods!

I started to include copies of *Eye on Local Nature* with my orders, explaining to John that we were collecting his birds in line with our bird identification proficiency.

Peter usually chose the bird of the month and, just before the Christmas of that year, wrote to Mr Waldon asking if he could interview him for the magazine. For some reason, we had assumed John was elderly (visions of the wood carver in Pinocchio I think) – and we were taken aback to be met by an energetic young man with a vast alsatian dog. The interview tells its own story – just imagine being *inside* a warm, wood-smelling cuckoo clock to share the enchantment of John's wood carving room:

JOHN WALDON – Master wood carver – talks about his work in an exclusive EYE ON interview, given to Peter

In a very hilly part of Bristol, in Clifton near Hotwells and the river, is a small house where master carver John Waldon lives.

When I knocked on the door, I was greeted by a friendly alsation dog as well as John. When I reached the workshop I was amazed – everywhere there were bird carvings, bird pictures, and long pieces of wood. The room itself was scattered with wood, and the walls were covered with tools of all kinds, and the floor with wood shavings. There were beautiful rafters forming the ceiling of the room. First, my interview;

Have you always had an interest in birds? Oh yes, ever since I was very young.

What made you take up bird carving? The first thing I did was to carve a housename

with birds on it, for friends. (John showed
me some lovely photographs of his early bird
house numbers).

How do you carve the birds for your brooches?
I draw them by hand onto strips, without using
a template, so that every one is different. Then I
cut them out using a fretsaw, carving with a scalpel.
My thumb gets pretty hardened!

What tools do you use?
I use a fretsaw and a scalpel. Then Fiona Williams
paints them (which she does beautifully!)

How long do the brooches take to make?
In an hour I can cut out a few of the same type.

What is your favourite place for Nature in Bristol?
Leigh Woods and the River Avon. I walk there every
day. There are very many types of duck on the river.

I believe you work for the Royal Society for the
Protection of Birds for part of the year?
Yes, for two years I have worked as a Species
Protection Warden, looking after rare breeding
birds.

BROOCHES
(actual size)

ROBIN

LONG
TAILED
TIT

We then had a closer look at some of John's bird
brooches which are beautifully carved - and then
painted by skilled painter, Fiona Williams.

The year which followed this happiest of issues was a fraught and sad one for our family, but no more, I know, than for thousands of others – loss and grief is part of family experience.

My mother died in this year, thirty-seven years after contracting multiple sclerosis, twenty of those years in almost complete paralysis. Mum died just a few months away from her fiftieth wedding anniversary. My father had promised her they would make that date. Every anniversary I heard him tell mum that they would make it to another year. My father doesn't believe in God. I do, because there has to be some way they can be together again.

The darkest of months for me, though, was always lit by the bravely continuing progress of *Eye on Local Nature*, by the kindness it was attracting to us all – and by the extraordinary adventures it generated for the boys. Living in a small flat in the centre of the city, Peter was beginning to have a part-time, almost fairy-tale country childhood.

RUNNING A MAGAZINE

Tracking down news for their magazine is the reason for almost every adventure that the boys – and we – have. Keith explains his side of the production work of the magazine in the appendix. It isn't difficult, but it's perhaps too detailed for inclusion here. Actual production is one half of the story, public relations is the other!

☐ Be as generous as you can with giving away copies to stimulate interest. We now charge 15p for *Eye on Local Nature*, adding the cost of postage where appropriate – but we give copies to anyone who writes for the magazine. I keep circulation records of addresses and when the next payment for postal subscribers is due. However, I do use my discretion about chasing up overdue subscriptions, and find people always do send money eventually! Peter has the money as his pocket money and lots of readers give him more than the 15p charged, telling him it's towards books and expenses!

☐ If you'd like the privilege of being taken seriously by professionals working in the field you choose, then it really does matter to take yourself seriously and to let children take themselves seriously. Children usually will unless they are made to feel self-conscious.

As Editors, the boys have had to deflect and resist a few 'silly' contributions – limericks, cartoons, irrelevant poetry. These offerings are well meant – and usually there's a serious observation behind them which is worth exploring instead.

☐ Illustrations can be a problem. Many children and adults can be persuaded to write for publication – most are terrified of drawing! Now, the boys and I do the illustrations and we prepare them for the next issue throughout the month – so there's no last minute rush and consequent temptation not to have pictures. Draw what you *see*. Start very small if it feels more comfortable.

☐ Many of their star scoops now come as a result of Peter and Matt writing to an expert with four questions written out, space left underneath for answers, a covering letter asking if the expert would kindly return the questionnaire, a complimentary copy of the magazine – and an SAE. Experts who have written books can be contacted c/o their publisher and the address will usually be in the front of the book. It's best if the questions are based on personal experience, curiosity and observation – and preferably not already answered many times over in the expert's published work! For younger children, though, a sure-fire question is to ask the expert how he/she became an expert or what is his or her favourite animal/place/tree/plant, etc. Literally no-one has ever refused to reply to the boys and some wonderful postal and personal friendships have been formed.

☐ 'Landmark' issues to celebrate six months, a year, two years of running – and Christmas – are a very important shot in the arm for a small magazine. Planning these keeps the interest high.

Part three
ADVENTURES

What *is* an adventure? I wonder if we are ever actually aware of adventure while it is happening? Afterwards, maybe. But in the present? Listen to children talking . . . 'Nothing *ever* happens around here . . . '

Can we agree that adventure is a time when something is discovered or something exciting and unexpected happens – however briefly? If we can agree on this, then believe me, there's nothing like the combination of Nature study and investigative journalism for this kind of adventure. Something always happens if you shed a little of the caution civilization breeds in us, look at surroundings curiously and with a magazine article in mind. Let me prove this by sharing some of *Eye on Local Nature*'s adventures.

The Wood Warden

In the adventure-seeking business you can't afford to be reticent or self-conscious. Peter tends to be both and so his magazine and Nature reporting are the best possible official reasons to be nosey. You're unlikely, I think, to encounter adventure while literally minding your own business – though it sounds more dramatic when related that way.

The boys' first adventure began on the slopes of the Avon Gorge, in the shady depths of Leigh Woods. The gentleman with whom we came face to face on one of the footpaths didn't look menacing, but the large, gleaming machete he carried certainly did. He passed us. Sighs of relief. We looked back. He stooped to pick up an old wheel hub by the side of the path and he looked back. Peter whispered, 'I think he knows what he's doing.'

I cannot remember exactly how the conversation began, but there is always a moment when curiosity is acknowledged, rejected or met by explanation. Mr Beazley explained that he was an official Nature Conservancy Council Voluntary Warden for the Leigh Woods Nature Reserve. We fell in beside him as he outlined what his duties were and, punctuating his conversation by bashing at brambles, told us how irritated he felt about having to retire as Assistant to Surrey's County Bee-keeping Instructor with years of 'go' left in him. That we could well believe.

We parted at a junction in the woods and noticed that Peter was rooted to the spot, doing battle with his shyness. Editorial responsibility won and he raced off after Mr Beazley, introduced himself as Editor of *Eye on Local Nature* and could he and Matt please interview Mr Beazley about being a Wood Warden? Mr Beazley gave us his address and that evening we posted him a copy of the magazine to establish good faith. This interview was to be different: the boys were to accompany Mr Beazley on his complete wardening round, to join in and see for themselves where it went and what it involved.

Matt and Peter were walked off their feet by this sprightly and determined gentleman. It was a long round and a bitterly cold January afternoon. The boys learned how Mr Beazley and a band of seven other Voluntary Wardens patrol the Reserve, keeping the footpaths clear of fallen trees and dangerous litter, watching out for the safety of the animal, plant and bird life – and making sure visitors to the Reserve didn't light fires, camp – or chop down trees!

It was impossible for the boys to make notes at the time – there was too much to see and do – and Mr Beazley set a rapid pace around the woods. We helped the children to record their impressions onto a cassette as soon as they were home and warmed up. To listen to them – the sudden rushes of words and details – and to hear us all interrupting each other with questions and facts is to capture and share adventure. The account of their afternoon with the Wood Warden was one of the most popular investigations undertaken by Peter and Matt. Circulation of the magazine soared!

There's a tremendous amount of curiosity about what wardening a National Nature Reserve actually involves. Patrolling the woods has about it a romantic, almost Robin Hood image. But we came to know more about this widespread curiosity – and even more about the minute by minute reality behind the image because, as a result of this adventure, we were soon to be serving our own probation as Voluntary Wardens for the Avon Gorge Reserve.

Waders!

As fundamental as curiosity to outdoor adventure is resistance to cold and wet. Some of us are simply more robust than others! Much of the resistance comes from good health, part of it from weatherproof clothing and food – and a significant proportion of this kind of stamina comes from the mind, from a complete absorption in what we are doing. Again, this may have to be worked on. Peter's keenest lesson in this kind of concentration came from John Waldon, the carver of my wooden bird brooches.

An estuary bird enthusiast, John offered to take Peter birdwatching. It proved so difficult to fix a mutual weekend date that we decided that Peter could take a day away from school rather than miss this opportunity. A day out with a bird expert like John was not to be missed on any account – and John was soon to leave Bristol to work as an RSPB Warden in Hampshire.

A day was settled, an agreement to go whatever the weather reached – but oh dear, what a day. It was even bitter cold indoors with the heating full on. Peter's article tells the story:

IN SEARCH OF WADERS: John Waldon of the RSPB
and Peter Taylor of Eye On Local Nature go in
search of Waders - John's favourite type of bird.

Report by Peter

I set off with John towards Portishead in
February - and about fifteen minutes later we
had reached the sea front. There was snow everywhere and as soon as I stepped out of the car, I
froze! The sea front was exposed and a cold wind
whipped mercilessly down upon us. We sheltered
in one of the beach shelters and John produced his
telescope. Straight away we spotted a curlew -

then several more - and some snipe pulling out
grubs with their long beaks. John said that
sometimes you cannot see snipe until you practica-
lly step on them - this is because they are so well
camouflaged among the yellowy grass of some mudflats.

Then, as we moved further along, we saw some
redshanks (with red legs) on the mud flats. All
the time as we were watching these birds, chaffin-
ches and pied wag-tails were flying across our line
of vision.

Later, we moved to a nearby pond and saw
mallard, pochard duck and even little grebe!
Also, we spotted a partial albino blackbird
with white patches on either side of its head.

I was pleased to have the chance to see the
waders, especially, and to readers who do not know
what these are, they are birds which in general
have a fat body on long legs, with a long bill and
they paddle around in the mud near rivers.

This was a small adventure with a lot of clout. Peter's most vivid
recollection was how John had seemed oblivious to the extreme cold
and wind. Eventually he had taken pity on Peter and they had moved
into a beach shelter with John's telescope – but Peter was lost in
admiration for this stoicism. He wanted to test himself against the
weather again.

Badgered by Peter and his friends, Keith – who has a lot of
sympathy for this kind of venture – started to organise a series of
'survival' adventures for local children. These adventures were
carefully graded to develop stamina and outdoor skills. The expedition to see waders in the middle of winter brought home the point that
to meet winter adventure bravely, you need a special depth of concentration – and an absorbing interest which keeps considerations of
comfort at bay.

The partial albino robin

To begin with, there were gentler adventures, too. Most haunting of these was the discovery of a partial albino robin (a robin with white markings) in Leigh Woods, and the mystery surrounding its long disappearance. I say gentler adventure, but there was, I remember, a good deal of drama at the time, and the story of this special robin touched the hearts of the magazine's readers. People love robins and the curiosity of these birds about human activities gives us the feeling that they return the affection.

The partial albino robin found us, in fact. It was January and we were desperately short of flowers to draw for the magazine. We had discovered a most peculiar pink flower called winter heliotrope which looks messy and quite horrid from a distance, but close up (and without competition from other flowers) is as lovely as its sweet smell. The biggest clump of blossoms was by the cottage of Mr and Mrs Bussell, tenants of the National Trust, who actually live in Leigh Woods.

Our breath forming a mist around us that frosty morning, Peter and I sat on the hard-frozen mud to choose a specimen of winter heliotrope to draw. A joyous burst of bird-song from the cottage garden made us both look up and there, a few feet away, on a bush, was 'Whitey' – a companionable robin with a pure white headscarf! 'Is it all right?' asked Peter. I didn't know either. 'I reckon it's having a bad moult,' Peter commented sympathetically, 'odd though. I've never seen a robin like *that* before.' Peter was, though, to see another robin like that sooner than he'd anticipated. However, this one was long dead and stuffed for posterity in the Bristol Museum. Matt and Peter had gone to the Museum to look round the Natural History Section again – and in a dark corner, among other pathetically preserved little birds, was the specimen: 'Partial Albino Robin: Brean Down, 22nd March 1961.' The markings on this curiosity were less extreme than Whitey's. Peter rocketed home to tell us that the bird wasn't moulting – it was *rare* and that someone had even shot the last one for the Museum!

The partial albino robin became the focus of our walks, to be greeted, studied and to be the subject of not very good photography. Best of all, the robin became a bridge to our friendship with the wood dwellers, Mr and Mrs Bussell. At first, Joe Bussell, who had spent 46 years in the woods, treated us with the suspicion and abruptness with which he faced all 'townee' visitors. Little by little, the reliability of our arrivals by his cottage and our obvious love of *his* robin Whitey began to commend us to him. Passers-by would watch puzzled as we sat, all three, staring and with binoculars trained into Mr Bussell's garden, our backs to the woods! But Joe Bussell shared our secret, and became, with his wife, close friends and a unique source of observation about wood life. We have sat in a remote part of the woods, well hidden, and suddenly been aware that Joe Bussell has walked past, silently, his slightly bow-legged figure and reflective manner as he treads the pathways he loves, transporting us back in time to another age and way of life.

And yet this slightly-built 80-year old is as brave as a bulldog – he'll tackle anyone and sometimes be attacked for it. When we first met him, he had recently returned from hospital after an attack.

However, one day in May, Mr Bussell met us outside his cottage with a sad face and with bad news: Whitey had gone. 'She's been with us two years or more,' Joe told me, 'and it was all over – just like that.' A sparrowhawk had flown across Joe's garden just after the robin had been seen on the birdtable. There was a tustle, the sparrowhawk had definitely taken a bird – and there were a few white feathers remaining in the garden. 'I'm sorry,' Joe said to Peter, 'Mrs Bussell's upset, too.'

Peter wrote a terse item for the magazine telling readers what had happened to Whitey. Back came letters telling us how sorry readers were. BBC producer Caroline Weaver wrote a special article:

THOUGHTS ON THE ALBINO ROBIN - by Caroline Weaver

I wonder whether the plight of the Albino Robin (issue 19) tells us something about evolution and natural selection? White is a very conspicuous colour and it may be a disadvantage for a woodland bird to be so, because it clearly stands out against the dull wood and green leaves. An aerial or ground predator can see them from a distance and pounce on them much more easily than on a brown bird. By being caught by a predator, a conspicuously col- oured bird is eliminated from the population. This

may be before it has a chance to lay its eggs, so
any offspring which might have been white are also
eliminated. So perhaps that's why we rarely see
white birds in our woods - natural selection has
weeded out the birds which are less able to survive.

A totally white bird with pink eyes is called a
true albino in the scientific world, and this char-
acteristic is genetically determined - that is,
inherited from its parents by a freak of nature.
But nowadays we see many familiar birds mottled
brown and white, or black and white (they are not
albinos). This is generally believed to be due to
the artificial and junk food they get in our gardens.
So this colouring is not due to inheritance, but
due to environment. If the young of these birds are
fed wholesome food they should exhibit the true
colours of the species - whether robin, blackbird
or thrush. So I'm sure it's worthwhile making sure
that we feed our garden birds wisely and don't offer
them waste or bad food.

One of Tony Soper's bird books will give anyone
interested a good guide as to how they can feed the
birds in their garden.

No amount of philosophy about the cruel laws of nature helped us
over the hurt of the loss of Whitey. Of course there were thousands of
other robins, equally lovable, but this one was special. However, once
before we had believed a special robin to be dead, and once before we
were proved wrong. And now, five months later, the partial albino
robin came home!

Mr Bussell was agitatedly on the lookout for us as we arrived at the
woods at our usual time. Whitey was home, he told us, he was *sure* it
was Whitey – please, could we come and see?

We perched in our usual spot for robin watching and waited. It was a
maddeningly long wait – then a burst of familiar song and Whitey
dropped into view, perched on a post in front of us and sang her heart
out. I nodded and put my thumbs up to Joe who rushed into his
cottage, and told Mrs Bussell, 'It *is* Whitey – they said it *is* Whitey!'
and there were tears of happiness in our eyes – for us, for the bird – and
for the Bussells.

The magazine was almost ready to print, but was re-written to incorporate news of the return of the partial albino robin. Again, readers wrote – this time to tell us their relief. Artist Robin Tanner wrote to Peter, 'We have heard – though this may not be true – that the females sometimes fly far away, even as far as France, in late summer, returning in autumn.'

We started a new tradition that Christmas. We went to Leigh Woods on Christmas day to sing carols to the Bussells and to the albino robin who watched us from the safety of her usual bush, fluffed up like a tennis ball in the cold of midwinter.

Orchids!

What other flowers can drive mankind to such a frenzy of possession? In the last century, plant hunters braved death to bring tropical orchids to Europe, stripping whole forests of these orchids, lest their rivals should find them! Now, mercifully, possession has been largely replaced by vigilant protection – but the near worship remains. I have heard of naturalists lying all night in beech woods training their torches over the woodland floor to absorb the more powerfully the atmosphere of the trembling white spectres of the rare ghost orchid. How can a plant inspire this awe? You simply have to see orchids, growing wild, incredible, hypnotic embodiments of plant beauty and intelligence, to understand. You can fall in love with a flower.

We had read of the Avon Gorge orchids and heard a rumour that an especially rare one – the bee-fly orchid – sometimes grew there. This actually meant little to us apart from fuelling our expeditionary ambitions for rarities, because we had never seen *any* orchids before – apart, of course, from the tarty, boxed orchids sold in florists.

Our orchid adventure began because we were curious – and this time we were nosey about what was fascinating to someone else. Pretending to be utterly absorbed in munching cheese rolls behind a rock on the side of the Avon Gorge, we watched a girl point a professional looking camera at something invisible to us, under a scrubby bush. Her boyfriend stood guard over the proceedings and frowned sternly in our direction. This went on for at least twenty minutes. Whatever was under that bush? We left, talking loudly and walked on for some way. Then, of course, when the coast was clear, we crept back to see for ourselves.

Goodness me. Love at first sight. It was a miracle on a stalk! Naturally we immediately jumped to the conclusion that we had stumbled across the rare bee-fly orchid. And we learned later from the University Botanic Garden that it was the less rare but equally wonderful wasp orchid – for the pink flower is a perfectly formed, life-size wasp – an incredibly ingenious device for luring real wasps onto the flower in an increasingly frustrated attempt to 'mate' with it. The

70

insect is, of course, being used by the orchid as a pollinator!

We had seen nothing like this before. Peter and Keith took photographs, taking care not to trample the grass down around the orchid and make it obvious to passers-by. The photographs were developed at once and Peter sent his prints to Dr Mark Smith, at the University Botanic Garden. (Peter and Matt had interviewed Dr Smith for *Eye on Local Nature* a few months previously and this extraordinary and generous man had started to write regularly for the boys' magazine.) Just one orchid was enough to compel us!

Once we knew what an orchid looked like (and the real thing in its setting is different from an illustration) we were able to find other orchids quickly and then, unexpectedly, we were able to horsetrade our 'expertise' with that of other orchid enthusiasts. Botanical knowledge of this kind becomes precious coinage.

On our next visit we found fly orchids – perfect *flies* on a stalk, richly and differently coloured in bands of red, brown and mauve. The fly detail and the black, shining eyes are miraculous. How does an orchid *know* what insects look like?

However, we knew that *somewhere* in the Avon Gorge was the location of the bee-fly orchid – a rare cross (hybrid) between the bee orchid and the fly orchid. We *had* to be close, surely. Once under the spell of orchids, the idea that there should be an area which contains such a rarity – or the possibility of such a rarity (for bee-fly orchids do not even occur every year) becomes an almost unbearable challenge. The flowering time of orchids is quite short – and we had only some evenings and weekends to search.

Four-leaf clover faith and a sizeable hint from Dr Smith were the keys. Following his hint, Dr Smith added, 'The hybrid between the bee and fly orchid . . . has never been found anywhere else in the world. There are only about three plants, and their great rarity means that their precise spot has to remain a secret'.

We had just enough information to go on and we ranged farther and farther into the Gorge in the roasting heat of an unprecedentedly hot summer. Then, by trying just one last path – we found our way into what I must describe with emotion as a paradise.

Through a dark, unhealthy wood, guarded by horrid black flies, through nettles and brambles, then out, dazzlingly into a hidden glade and there – dainty common spotted orchids growing as freely as bluebells, huge twayblade like little green pegs on stalks, fly orchids growing so profusely that we had to watch each footfall – and one perfect, exotic bee orchid. A bejewelled bee, offering itself to the sun. Surely this had to be the bee-fly orchid place?

But we were not alone. Two gentleman with cameras appeared to be quite at ease in paradise. We supposed that they too were orchid seekers – but this, of course, had to be established. We were by now fiercely protective of what we had found. We exchanged pleasantries on the hot weather and the blue sky, on the general abundance of wild flowers – and all wondered if there would be a drought this year. Conversation was grinding to a halt. This was getting nowhere. I decided to take a risk and ask them if they would identify an orchid for me, leading them to the large bee orchid.

They had actually overlooked this specimen, were delighted, and in return they led us to a hybrid which they studied whenever they came to Bristol in orchid season. Here was dedication indeed, for the tatty hybrid (a cross between a fragrant and a common spotted orchid) was not much to look at. They were, they explained, in Bristol for an orchid convention and, having spent most of the time discussing and examining bee orchids, what they badly wanted but couldn't find, were *wasp* orchids. Here we could help and horsetrading began. I raised the question of the bee-fly orchid and, stressing its rarity (orchid lovers fly in from around the world when there has been an official sighting) the gentlemen also confirmed that we had indeed found the bee-fly place. None of us knew the *exact* spot, however.

Peter was overawed by all this, especially as their expertise so heavily outweighed ours – we were beginners of two weeks at orchids. He hesitantly explained that he was an Editor of *Eye on Local Nature* and asked the gentlemen if they would write an article about orchids. They were reluctant – orchid enthusiasts are justifiably secretive – but they gave us their address so that we could send them a copy of the magazine. We had been out in the heat for hours and were exhausted and getting ratty. However, on the long trek home we found an even lovelier wasp orchid than the one we had first seen and debated what to do. Should we go back – a long way – to tell the gentlemen about our find, or press on home to get cool. We ran back. The orchid enthusiasts loved our new specimen (it had an unusually curly wasp-tail) and, I suppose in reward, *Eye on Local Nature* eventually received a long article about orchids from one of the gentlemen.

Before I describe how we made total fools of ourselves over the bee-fly in the year following, I must explain how Peter's photograph of a wasp orchid lured a local genius to our front door. In fact, this is the way things happen in Nature study. A letter to one expert will capture the attention of another: whole networks are forged in this way.

Some time after Peter had sent his wasp orchid photograph to Dr Mark Smith, the Editors of *Eye on Local Nature* received this letter:

Dear Peter and Matt,

I have read some of your *Eye on Local Nature*s and I have found them very good.

I have been working at the University Botanic Garden, under Mark Smith for three years. During this time I have become especially interested in British orchids.

I was very excited when I saw the picture of Ophrys apifera 'trollii' (wasp orchid) that you sent to Mark Smith for identification. I knew the wasp orchid grew in the Avon Gorge but not in the thin section of grass. There was a group of nine this year.

I would be very grateful if you could spare a copy of the wasp orchid photograph. I would be willing to pay for a copy.

I have found quite a few different species of orchids over the last few years. This includes the elusive fly orchid and a fairly rare helleborine.

I would be delighted if I could accompany you on walks looking for orchids. I know a few other sites where orchids grow. One such site, the other side of Bristol, had about 250 spikes of pyramidal orchids and about 25 flowering spikes of bee orchids. The site is unusual as it is on a main road, used by heavy traffic.

Yours sincerely,

Trevor Baker

It was too late that year to go on any more orchid hunts, but Peter sent Trevor regular copies of the magazine – and we formed a comfortable mental picture of Mr Baker as a middle-aged, reticent and probably a little stooping gardener, whose friendship was likely to be valuable – and a bit dull.

The reality was wonderfully different. Trevor, who arrived on our doorstep some months later, badger skull in hand, is an utterly charming, bouncy, fair-haired youngster in his late teens. Trevor Baker lives on one of Bristol's toughest council estates, with his terrier, lurcher and ferrets – and he is, in his way, a genius. That is not just how we view him. For three years, until Dr Smith died at the tragically early age of 50, Trevor was his protégé at the University Botanic Garden.

I wouldn't have believed in someone like Trevor unless I'd met him and lived through some of the adventures he effortlessly conjured for us. Trevor can charm birds out of the trees, badgers out of their setts – and probably plants out of the ground! Certainly his homing instincts on the unusual far outweighed mine. Thanks to Trevor we have seen carpets of blue anemones in the wild, gasped at the unearthly beauty of fritilleries growing where we would never have found them, wandered through oceans of bluebells hidden behind a city rubbish dump, opened our eyes to many other orchids, been with badgers in the woods – and learned more about on-the-spot fieldcraft in two hours than our experience had taught us in several years.

Thanks too, to Trevor, we have lost our squeamishness about badger dung pits, have dissected fox scats (droppings) to see what the animal had eaten the night before ('You'll need warm water to dissolve it', Trevor advised Peter, thrusting a plastic bag full of droppings into my hand) and have learned to live with a badger skull in the bedroom and a lesser horseshoe bat pickled in a bottle in the kitchen.

The evening Trevor came to introduce himself, he explained that he was away from work with a perforated eardrum, having slipped on recent ice and got a shrub stuck in his ear. He'd been spending the time walking about during the week and it was incredible what he had seen – how much bolder the wildlife was when there were less people about. Should he write an article for the magazine about it?

The conversation inevitably turned to orchids – and we described our hunt for the bee-fly, explaining that we didn't really know what it looked like. Was it like a bee orchid or a fly orchid? Trevor hadn't seen it either, but knew it was a *wider* fly orchid – the wing part at the bottom was rounder, like a bee. Fly orchids are usually quite stream-lined. He'd come along with us when we went searching next year . . .

So now we knew to look hard at the fly orchids. I think we expected some exotic, transforming experience. Peter imagined the top half of a fly with the bottom half of a bee. I hoped for pink petals like a halo around an especially voluptuous fly. We associated rarity with beauty. We should by now have known better; rarity is valued for its own sake.

But the following year was not a spectacular year for orchids in the Avon Gorge. There were a good number of fly orchids – in fact, the BBC came out to film them – but there were far fewer bee and wasp orchids. Pity, we thought. So this won't be the year to find the hybrid. And we searched on, all three of us, in a lower gear, ceasing to believe in the impossible.

It was a weekday morning in midsummer and Peter was at school. The heat build-up in the Gorge was incredible and Keith and I had been systematically searching for three hours. There was little shade and we had been out of tea for some time. It was a long way home, and we couldn't bear the heat any longer; the skin on my arms was burning and both of us were wet with sweat.

We headed for home. But as we left the area, we met a team of three marching in – a woman and two men. Both the men were carrying very expensive cameras and what Keith whispered to me was 'state of the art macro!' for close-up photography.

'They've got £800 worth of equipment round their necks,' he added enviously. By now we were official Wardens for the Nature Conservancy Council – but not on this side of the Gorge. Deciding to bluff, we put our official Warden armbands on and confronted the party on the path, 'Have you come to see the orchids?' They looked at Keith's armband and replied 'We've come to see the bee-fly.'

'Do you know where it is?' I asked incredulously, 'Yes – we've seen it,' the woman replied, trekking on purposefully.

Once they had passed us, we started to laugh. This was the joke of the week. They'd come to see the bee-fly, just like that! Good luck to them! And we laughed all the way back to the motorbike, and, under our helmets, all the way home.

I stopped laughing at 2 am the next morning. I couldn't sleep and fly orchids were crawling up the wallpaper all round the room. What had we *done*? Why had we assumed that because *we* couldn't find it that it wasn't there! Such arrogance! Were we mad? 'I'm not turfing out of bed *now* with a searchlight,' mumbled Keith unhelpfully when I woke him up to explain my conclusion that the bee-fly orchid was there and we'd just thrown away the best chance we'd ever have to see it. But it would be dawn in a few hours, and I went downstairs to make some sandwiches.

For three hours in the morning and three hours in the relative cool of the late afternoon, we searched the area – up every rock, along every path, inching forward gently and gingerly on our hands and knees. Every fly orchid looked slightly different. Peter and I did battle with an evil thorn bush to look at an orchid underneath it. The markings were certainly unusual – but it didn't have a wide rear. It was maddening.

Then Keith found an orchid which had been knocked over and carefully propped up with an unobtrusive twig. Furthermore, the whereabouts of this flower was indicated by a white tissue and a plastic cup which had not been there the day before. Amateur botanists often do this silly kind of landmarking to remind themselves where to look. On the other hand, we had learned that other botanists do it to throw fellow enthusiasts off the scent . . . Was anything different about this orchid?

We peered and peered and yes, the saddle at the bottom was wider than usual. 'It looks a bit like Mr Tumnus the Faun in *The Lion, the Witch and the Wardrobe*', Peter commented. But otherwise it looked a perfectly normal brown fly orchid with a blue stripe across it. Peter photographed it – and a few others for comparison – and we began the long journey home.

Once home, we telephoned Trevor Baker – but he was out fishing. We telephoned one of the orchid experts we had encountered the previous year. Yes, he had seen a photograph of the bee-fly and told us it had a blue stripe and a wider lip at the bottom. If we had seen it this year, he would come to Bristol at once. We rushed him a copy of the photograph.

We were beginning to understand that the bee-fly may be botanically amazing, but it wasn't likely to be visually any more startling than a fly orchid. But investigative botany was taking on an almost unbearable urgency. Was it or wasn't it the bee-fly? The orchids were beginning to wither – it would soon be too late to tell.

Having seen Peter's photograph, the University Botanic Garden was not sure one way or the other. Trevor decided to take the matter in hand and took the photographs to the Bristol Museum Records Department who were compiling a new Bristol Flora. The Museum at once pronounced the orchid as the bee-fly. It was to go in the new Bristol Flora as a sighting by Peter Taylor and Co. And it was a very brief moment of glory.

Later that week, our orchid expert friend telephoned. He was sorry, but it wasn't the bee-fly. He'd seen many slightly wider bottomed fly orchids like that in Kent. It simply wasn't wide enough. He would go on checking with his even more expert contacts, but we should assume it wasn't the bee-fly unless we heard from him again in the next few days. And we didn't.

Badgers

If we found orchids because we were curious, our fascination with badgers started because we were restless. Peter wanted to explore farther into the woods. He had, he reckoned, learned to navigate by compass and one day in the summer holidays he told me that however far we went into the woods, he could navigate us safely back. 'O.K.,' I said, pocketing a safety whistle, 'let's go get lost . . . '

Once over the suspension bridge and into Leigh Woods, we left our usual route and entered the more confusing and daunting depths of the adjoining Bristol Forest. I think I can navigate here by feel: I don't mean instinct, but I can sense the slight slope of the land down to the Avon Gorge. Even so, we were wandering far from known territory. Then, in one of the startlingly light glades which occur in this forest, we found a bank of familiar clover-like apple green leaves – the leaves of the beautiful wood sorrel. It's a delicate, wistful white flower, not widely known, and by the spread of the leaves, this little bank would be a paradise in the spring – marvellous to photograph.

That was enough of a find for us. Peter navigated us back to Mr Bussell's cottage and our priority was to take Keith to show him our sorrel bank. We'd drawn a sketch plan of the area – with tree and glade landmarks so that we could find it again when we took him.

And so we started regular and more adventurous forays into Bristol Forest, making mental notes of all the leaves which told us what would be blossoming there in the spring – and thrilled that here was an even richer source of plant life. But not only plant life because suddenly, about 2 metres away from a path and under a large, dark yew tree, Keith found an enormous badger sett. We had only seen pictures of setts before and were astonished at its size and complexity, finding hole after hole – 17 in all – in the lumpy ground. We also found two rotten wooden slats, nailed up a tree overlooking the sett and this, presumably, once made a hide for an observer or photographer.

Goodness knows why we all loudly agreed that of course there weren't any actual badgers here – that the sett was probably long abandoned. I suppose the idea of an occupied badger sett on this vast scale was too much to hope for! On the other hand, Peter and I had both noticed some grey 'stuff' in small holes a little way apart from the sett – and wondered if it was badger dung. Peter made a diagram of the sett for the magazine and we announced to the readers the find of a 'Badger Ghost Town'.

I brought home an armful of books on badgers from the City Library, including several by one of the country's leading authorities on badgers – Dr Ernest Neal MBE (later to be a writer for *Eye on Local Nature*). These books made riveting reading – far more gripping than any detective story. We learned what to look out for – and went back to our ghost town.

We knelt down in the mud and, by gently sifting through some of the loose mud and fibres at the entrance to the holes, we found badger hairs – first one (great excitement and yet still some scepticism), then another and eventually so many that we took them for granted! These hairs were wiry and sometimes in three colours – white, ginger-brown and black on the same hair. The hairs were about 6–8 cm long. We found what looked like bedding – grass, leaves and hay – thrown out of the sett. First I, then Peter put our heads into the badger holes and sniffed. We could certainly smell something musty.

We'd also read about badger dung pits – little holes for dung just away from the main sett. These were easy to find – and fresh looking wet dung was filling the small holes, surrounded by large, evil looking red-backed flies which flew around the holes and the bedding. Other dung pits showed us that the badgers had been feasting on the red berries of the yew tree.

There was no longer any room for doubt. This sett was 'live'. 'Think of them down there,' commented Peter, 'wondering what we're up to, up here!' For us this was a wonderful discovery; it was the first time we had been so close to badgers in the wild. Matt came out to see the sett and the two Editors kept their readership informed of each new discovery.

We began to make plans to go to the forest at dusk to watch for badgers, but by now it was midwinter. The sett was far into the forest, navigating back would be a nightmare and so the expedition was something to be talked about rather than done for the moment.

Meanwhile, we went on reading about badgers. We learned that badgers scratch their claws on 'scratching trees' which also mark their territories. Matt and Peter set themselves to finding a scratching tree. Several trees around the sett had substantial chunks of bark missing from their bases – but bark was also missing from higher up, pointing to the likelihood of squirrel rather than badger activity. We didn't then know that badgers can climb trees a little way. But the special trees were there, and goodness knows how we missed them at first. A tree on either side of the main entrance to the sett: both trees deeply and conclusively gored.

Radiating from the sett were little paths, too small to have been made by humans, leading in all directions through the undergrowth, under fallen trees, narrowly through nettles – and far off into the forest. We followed these paths and found three equally enormous badger setts, all with the same signs of occupation and some with paw and claw marks in the soft earth. In one of these setts, the badgers had excavated an awesome amount of limestone rock – and next door to the badgers' home were the remains of a hut, a kettle, a pair of toeless boots and a sock. Someone had been living alongside the badgers.

A letter from Trevor Baker told the boys that the setts of the size described in the magazine would have been in occupation for a hundred years or so. Mr Bussell confirmed that one of the setts – romantically named 'The Badger Sett by the Cowslip' had been in use throughout the 46 years he had lived in the woods. Once, too, there was a field of cowslips. Now only a precious one remains.

The retired Ranger, Cecil Baker, another 80-year old still living in one of the cottages in the woods, told us of his own trip-wire and magnesium flash efforts to photograph the animals – how he and his friends would set up the equipment, spend the evening at the local public house and then return to see what they had captured on film.

We longed to see badgers. Just to stand at the junction of those little paths gave us the thrilling vision of badgers at nightfall, emerging from their holes one by one, sniffing the air and heading out along one of the tiny paths, snuffling for food and ready for action.

Trevor Baker came to our rescue. Badgers? He knew all about badgers. Once he'd crawled right into a hole and got stuck and had to be pulled up again by his feet. He'd had to release a live badger from a trap, once, too. It hadn't been a bit grateful. But he seriously advised us against examining the stomach contents of a dead badger to see what it had been eating (authorities on badgers sometimes encourage enthusiasts to embark on this kind of pathology). He'd tried it once on a fox and it wasn't very nice . . . But if we wanted *badgers*, Trevor assured us, it was no trouble at all.

However, things didn't always go according to plan – even for

Trevor. He arrived on our doorstep after work, a big bag full of Nature books for Peter ('Got any use for these? I've run out of space in my bedroom.') and a sad story. Trevor's brother had found a dead badger on the road on his way to work in the meat department of the local supermarket. Knowing that Trevor was coming to see Peter that night to talk about badgers, he wondered if he should take the badger with him and keep it in the meat cold store. Possibly not. He hid the corpse under a bush, intending to lash it to the back of his motorbike with elastic ropes and bring it home at the end of the day. But when he returned, the body had gone. (I now take it for granted that naturalists are on the look out for badger corpses.) So Trevor's apologies. He'd meant to bring along a dead badger for us to study in the kitchen. Not to worry, though. He'd soon get another. Would a fox be of interest too?

'About now would be a good time to see badgers,' Trevor told us at the end of August. 'I've found somewhere for you.' Yet even then we didn't really expect to see much. Friends had just returned, disappointed, from a luckless expedition with a professional naturalist. Keith said he was expecting only to see the hind quarters of something disappearing at 90 mph behind a bush. We should, of course, have known better. Trevor was in charge of *our* expedition.

On the day of the watch, I made up red torches (badgers don't see red light – you can, the books say, shine it right at them) using a piece of car reflector I picked up in the road. I didn't make any sandwiches because even we realised we couldn't munch sandwiches and drink tea while waiting for badgers to emerge. The animals are short sighted but are sensitive to the very slightest sound or smell.

At 7.30 pm we met up outside a local pub of Trevor's choice and headed out of Bristol, over the motorway, through farmlands down hills and on and on, deep into 'Trevor's country'. Trevor stopped his brisk pace now and then to show us rabbit runs (worn patches where the rabbits run out of scrub and bushes and – more to the point – where they run quickly back!) 'This field is full of rabbits watching us right now,' Trevor remarked. We became adept at spotting the tunnel-like runs into the brambles. 'It's better than *Watership Down*,' whispered Peter, crouching down to peer along a tunnel.

Over fields, down banks – how on earth, I wondered, are we going to get back over this terrain later on in the pitch black? Were we going to be out all night? I was starving already and longing for a cup of tea. On and on, under wire, over gates.

Then Trevor's manner changed. He became quieter and more cautious. He indicated the wood. We pushed gently into it, the half-darkness of dusk like an irritating veil in front of our eyes. We tried to tread silently but bluebell seed-cases crackled alarmingly under our feet. 'Try to be quiet now,' warned Trevor, 'I've brought you in so the wind is in your faces and they can't smell you – but we don't want them hearing you. They're nobody's fool. There's two setts and we'll be sitting between them.'

At this precise point, my ankle turned and I fell heavily down the slippery bank. That's it, I thought, I've ruined the expedition. But Trevor seemed unperturbed. He motioned us to sit down and we sat down in a row, Peter with Trevor, Keith with me. Keith slipped down into the sleeping position, anticipating a long wait. Peter hissed to Keith to stop breathing like a steam engine – and then Peter started twiddling his thumbs maddeningly. Throughout Trevor sat patiently, silent and unmoving.

After a short time, I began to find the falling darkness hypnotic and learned to ease my position every time the wind blew through the trees and masked the noise of my movements. Without warning there was an incredibly loud crashing sound then a series of bloodcurdling mewing screams. Trevor turned to us and mouthed 'cubs'. I saw two shapes in a tunnel of light high up the bank above us in the wood. Badgers were here!

We went on waiting, straining our eyes in all the directions where loud clumpings could be heard. Trevor had told us that badgers just crash about in the undergrowth, 'They've no bushcraft'. But *so* loud? It was like being surrounded by dinosaurs – hearing them, but desperate for proof. The waiting went on.

And then – agony! A stinging insect (and heaven forbid that I dwelt on exactly *what*) crawled up the leg of my jeans and started to bite. Every time I thought I'd squashed it by rubbing my hand noiselessly against my leg, the insect crawled off and started to bite me somewhere else. Keith eased himself into the sitting up position and Peter hissed at him to shush. There was a noise to one side. Trevor motioned Peter to look for a snout. I could see only a shape moving quickly against what was left of the light.

As night fell, the wood became even noisier. Owls hooted, wood pigeons took off, clattering through the trees; small insects crawled over the crackly undergrowth. Moths and creepy-crawlies flew round and into us. The insect up my leg was still biting away. It was getting

81

colder and the wind was squalling through the trees, knocking trunk against trunk.

Then, very close to us – a loud clump, clump, clump. We shone red torches in the direction of the noise, and there – incredibly, a badger's head. It was astonishingly white and black and looking straight at us, so close! Surely it must take fright soon? The tension was unbearable – yet the badger went on staring, the torches reflecting a pinkish red in its eyes. He was a beautiful, glossy smart fellow – and in no hurry to be off! We were with a badger on his own territory, his land – and the woods took on a new perspective, wild, mysterious, wonderful.

After the badger eventually retreated, we went on training our torches wherever we heard noises, until these clumpings ceased, and Trevor whispered that they'd moved off for the night. We stumbled, groped and fumbled our way out of the wood. We'd done it! We'd been with badgers in the wild!

Something strange is falling out of the sky

It *is* possible to have an adventure with trees – and this time our involvement became part of a nationwide concern for the future of our beloved English oaks. It was Mr Bussell who brought us the news that something awful was happening in the woods. On the fourth of September 1983, Peter, Keith and I sat on the log opposite his cottage, watching for the partial albino robin and drinking our tea. Mr Bussell ambled towards us more purposefully than usual, waving his arms about, and told us that something strange was falling out of the sky. 'One of 'em fell right on my head and bounced off!' He'd caught one of the evil little lumps, he told us, and realised it had started life as an acorn. Anyway, he'd put one by to show us, but he couldn't for the life of him find where he'd put it.

We knelt down on the ground under the oaks and peered. I found a peculiar, messy conglomeration – heavy and ugly like the palm of a small, deformed green hand. 'That's one,' said Mr Bussell, 'the little devils are all over the place.' He reckoned that the long hot summer had not allowed the acorns a chance to 'set' – but even so, Mr Bussell admitted, there had been other long hot summers, even hotter, and he'd never seen anything like it in his 46 years in the woods. It was horrible.

We checked the other oak trees we knew in Leigh Woods and at least half seemed affected in this way. We didn't make a particularly scientific investigation, unfortunately, because we were inclined to accept Mr Bussell's view about the long hot summer – and we didn't know enough about the varieties of oak trees to distinguish which types were bewitched by this deformity.

I brought three 'acorns' home and sliced up two with a scalpel but we couldn't find anything inside, or any other clue as to what was wrong. The conglomerations were slimy and vile, and only a pathetic corner of the acorn cup was visible. It looked for all the world like the mess when an egg cracks and spills out in boiling water.

While I was cutting up the two specimens on the kitchen table, Peter wrote to Mr May of *The Times*, drawing a life-sized deformed acorn. After this, we found the horrid lumps under English oaks everywhere we looked – but we heard nothing more of the phenomenon until Mr May told *The Times* readership about the plight of the acorns in his *Nature Notes* of 26th September:

> The ground under many oak trees is strewn with acorns affected by knopper gall, which is produced by the grubs of small gall-wasps feeding inside them. The acorns are scarcely recognisable; they are coated with greasy-looking black and brown spikes, as if bewitched.

The following week, Mr May commented on the implications for wildlife: 'The oaks are full of woodpigeons feeding on the green acorns that have escaped the malformations of knopper gall.'

Meanwhile, Mr Bussell had consulted us about a distressed wood pigeon which, bloated and unable to fly, was hiding in a patch of nettles near his cottage. Was it dying after eating a deformed acorn? Were these nasty lumps dangerous to wildlife in addition to depriving them of their usual foodstock? We were stumped. We didn't know.

Then, in the middle of October, *The Times* published an article entitled, *Friends of the mighty oak hunt down insect enemy* and we learned that the workings of knopper gall had far-reaching implications as there are no insect enemies to keep it in check. Our oaks were in serious trouble. The article showed Dr Michael Crawley of Imperial College, briefing a group of youngsters who had collected in London to take part in what the paper described as the biggest acorn hunt in history – to find out how many of London's oaks had been attacked by the little insect, Andricus quercuscalicis. Dr Crawley was explaining that this insect will not only threaten the long-term future of the oak – but also deprive jays, pigeons, squirrels and wood mice of their usual autumn food.

We wrote at once to Dr Crawley, enclosing a copy of *Eye on Local Nature* and telling him our observations in the Leigh Woods region – and asking about the bloated pigeon. We asked him what we could actually *do* to help? I had just posted the letter when Peter rushed out of the front room to tell me Dr Crawley was on television saying that the knopper gall situation was grave and widespread.

Dr Crawley promptly replied to our letter:

> I was most interested to see the Leigh Woods Nature notes; I am a regular visitor myself to see the Avon wild flowers. Mr Bussell's view that the 'deformity' of the acorns was due to the dry summer, is quite widespread,

in fact. The galls are, however, produced by the oak tree in response to genetic messages injected to the plant by the insect when it lays its egg. The plant then produces a growth with acts as both a house and a restaurant for the developing grub!

Your estimate of 70% attack is most useful; are you certain that all the oaks you looked at were *Quercus robur*, for I have never seen the knopper gall on *Quercus petraea* or any of its hybrids.

Obviously the weather conditions this year must have been particularly favourable for the gall wasp. I also think that the insect has now become thoroughly adapted to British conditions, and is increasing to the carrying capacity of its environment, which is set, in this case, by the number of acorns produced each year. I do not think that the galls are toxic to squirrels; these animals open up a number of the galls to eat the insect living inside. The best thing naturalists can do is to gently heel into the ground any English oak acorns they find . . .'

Thank goodness there was something we could advise *Eye on Local Nature*'s readers to do – we could all push English acorns into the ground in the tradition of the sea captains who spent much of their time on land planting acorns (for future ships) from a stock carried around in their pockets! Peter explained to the readers that our oaks were in trouble and asked them to help us in planting acorns.

In time, of course, Dr Crawley was to write for Peter and Matt's magazine, joining the many botanical consultants to whom we turned for illumination when faced with the more outlandish peculiarities such as the unfathomable ways of cuckoo pint – or the case of the four-headed celandine! However, this adventure brought with it a new development, because Dr Crawley began to actually ask *us* for information.

To be asked for help by a professional is enough to make any amateur naturalist light-headed. Unfortunately, Dr Crawley's first request stumped us:

Have any of your readers noted brood parasitism by common garden birds; a female acting 'cuckoo like' and laying her eggs in the nest of another bird? Observations of a bird evicting eggs of its own species might be the first evidence of this process.

I stalked the nesting sparrows and blackbirds vainly watching for signs of peculiar behaviour. It seemed an undesirable development in birds, but even so it was annoying to have nothing to report.

Dr Crawley's next request was for more observations about knopper gall and Peter and I determined to get to grips with it – and to get the necessary information. In 1984 knopper gall continued, though fortunately less so. Dr Crawley wrote to us:

> The knopper gall continues to provide us with interesting ecological puzzles. The rate of attack on acorns this year is well down on last year's peak (under 30% compared with over 90%), despite the fact that the acorn crop is roughly the same size. It turns out that this reduction in wasp numbers is not to do with the native oak, but with the early spring generation which the wasps spend on the male flowers in the Turkey oak. Because there were so many galls on the ground last autumn, we expected very high numbers of galls on the Turkey oak (about twice as many as in the previous year, or thereabouts).
>
> What actually happened, was that we only got *one tenth as many* galls this year as last on the male flowers. We have no idea why this dramatic crash occurred; the insects emerged successfully from the knopper galls, they had their full complement of eggs etc. This March was colder and less sunny than 1983, and there was less wind, so perhaps dispersal by flight was impaired. It would be interesting if your readers could let us know whether oaks close to Turkey oaks had higher rates of galling this year, as this might help us sort out whether dispersal difficulties were the main cause. Alternatively, the development of the Turkey oak buds may have been delayed, so that the wasps were short of suitable places to lay their eggs when they arrived on the Turkey oaks. As ever, any information you could send us would be greatly appreciated . . . '

At first, Peter and I found this request daunting. We read the letter over and over again before were understood what we were asked to do. We were to look at English oaks next to Turkey oaks (the acorns of the Turkey oak are borne in very mossy, green cups – and the leaves are thinner and longer) and we were to report if these English oaks were worse affected by the knopper gall deformity than English oaks not in proximity to Turkey oaks.

We located one English oak next to Turkey oaks in Leigh Woods, with the help of the retired Ranger, Cecil Baker – who had planted many of the trees in the local woodland! This was not really conclusive however. We had to do better. Where else could we go?

Then Peter remembered that years ago, on one of our visits to the original clump opposite Bristol Zoo, we had noticed how many different types of oak tree there were – and collected different acorns. Perhaps if we went back to the clump . . . and perhaps the robin would still be there?

It was a sad visit. Much of our clump had been ravaged by the mowing machines, shrubs torn up and burnt. The Corporation was reclaiming our clump, taming it to the neatness of parkland. Discouraged, we didn't wait for the robin – but we did look at the trees. Here, Turkey oaks outnumbered English oaks, surrounding them, branches intertwined with them. And the deformity of the English oak acorns was terrible, almost like science-fiction in its menacing repulsiveness. We were glad to leave.

Peter and I put our observations together and composed a sober, scientific reply:

10th September 1984

Dear Dr Crawley,

Thank you very much for your letter about knopper gall. We have sent copies to various wildlife organisations and will be printing it in the October *Eye on Local Nature*.

Meanwhile, we have investigated the proportions of knopper gall – and especially those oaks near to Turkey oaks.

Six Quercus robur oaks in the Leigh woods area are affected very lightly. As far as we could see with binoculars, I would say that the proportion of affected acorns is less than 30%. There was no Turkey oak in the immediate vicinity.

The retired Ranger, Mr Cecil Baker, took me to a robur growing near (next to) two Turkey oaks. The robur was growing in deep shade. Again, using binoculars, I could see that a higher proportion of acorns was affected: 50% at least. But overall this robur had fewer acorns than elsewhere observed in Leigh Woods.

However, this morning, Peter and I went to an area of Bristol Downs where there are more Turkey oaks than English oaks. Here the picture was different. There were many (8) English oaks surrounded by, or touching Turkey oaks. In *every* case, the proportion of affected acorns was much higher – and certainly even higher than last year. It was difficult to find perfectly formed acorns on these trees and they had some of the most hideously deformed acorns we have yet seen.

We posted our report in the hope that our tiny piece of local observation in the hands of the professional researchers will do something to help the oak, the king of our trees. And, of course, we will go on planting acorns.

FAMILY ADVENTURES

Adventure is a frame of mind – it's difficult to be theoretical about it!

☐ Curiosity is vital. Watch other people – follow them even. If we meet people who look as interested in the details of their surroundings as we are, we ask them why they are there and what they are looking for. Collectors, flower pickers and plant uprooters are the enemy, of course. Empty hands – or notebooks and cameras are tokens of good faith.

☐ Detailed local knowledge, even of a very small locality, is your coinage as an amateur. If you meet experts visiting your area, you may find that although they have the technical expertise, you have the highly-prized on-the-spot knowledge. This is a potent combination for adventure.

☐ We always carry a pencil and paper to swap addresses and telephone numbers. Peter designed his own compliments slip with address and telephone number for this purpose.

☐ Follow up contacts quickly, especially if information has been promised or a further meeting suggested.

☐ One of the party must be able to navigate and map-read. It's hard to concentrate if you are afraid of getting lost – or if your mind is preoccupied with remembering the way you came, so that you can get home. For safety, we carry whistles. Six long, well-spaced blasts, repeated at intervals of one minute is the International Distress Signal. Probably few people would realise or react to this in practice, but at least the police would eventually respond to it if they had to come searching. When I go to the woods exploring, or on wardening patrol alone, I leave a note on the kitchen table saying where I've gone, the time I left and when I expect to get home.

☐ Adventures don't come in measured paces or at convenient times – although we usually manage to confine ours to the weekends! However, you have to be prepared to juggle priorities and act quickly while enthusiasm is fresh. If I have ever tried to postpone

88

an adventure, our roof springs a leak or a friend in distress arrives on the doorstep. Adventures are lost for ever this way.

☐ If there's an adventure brewing, I'll ask if Peter can have time away from school. His secondary school is understanding, even encouraging about his time off for conservation matters. Keith takes his annual leave in small doses so he too can act on impulse.

☐ I'm trained in first aid which means that I can the more confidently accept responsibility for the other children who join our adventures. First aid societies hold frequent local courses – and their joint manual (The St John Ambulance, The British Red Cross Society and St Andrew Ambulance Association) is available from any bookshop.

☐ Our adventures in the Bristol area are in the lowlands (ie under 300 metres – 1000 ft). Upland and remote areas need special care and are not really suitable for young children.

Part four
INVESTIGATIONS

The hooded mystery

From our knopper gall correspondence with Dr Crawley of Imperial College, we understood that professional naturalists would take it for granted that we were familiar with the Latin classification of living things. Trevor Baker's encyclopaedic knowledge and persuasive Bristolian Latin pronunciation made this sound deceptively easy, 'Say the Latin name to yourself while you look at the plant,' he explained, 'just keep saying it over and over. You'll get it.' Once we'd mastered two or three Latin names for wild flowers we felt quite superior and kept using them all the time. It does get easier.

By now, too, we were in a bit of a frenzy of information gathering, unable to resist all the requests to take part in surveys held by the Nature organisations we'd joined. Just about every Nature club and society is surveying and analysing habitats, hedgerows, pond life, frogspawn in cities, butterflies, nesting birds, migratory birds, woodland birds, birds of prey, garden birds, cuckoos . . . This was, of course, useful practice for us and, I hope, of help to the organisations concerned. Sometimes, though, rifling through all the forms to tick the appropriate list at the correct time was turning Nature study for me (and I usually carry the forms around) into a branch of the Civil Service.

It wasn't long, therefore, before we found a new way to look at investigations. We discovered that it's much more fun to be in charge of them now and then – sending people scrambling over the countryside in search of the information *we* wanted – and most illuminating of all: it's the information and curiosities the surveys *don't* ask for that fuels adventure and transforms scientific infor-mation-gathering into a series of compellingly romantic episodes.

Birds, animals and plants don't always conform to the 'average' any more than do human beings. Plants, for example, can be unpre-dictable and individualistic. Flowers aspire to be prima donnas and experiment with colour, adding extra petals to their finery for good measure. Others turn delinquent and sprout four heads on a single stalk. Yet more shy to minute proportions – or egotistically plump to

93

gross exaggerations of their textbook size. There's more to surveys than meets the eye . . .

Our first full-scale survey started because the variations in one plant, cuckoo-pint, puzzled us. Cuckoo-pint would puzzle anyone – it's odd by all standards, as Peter's diagram of the open 'flower' demonstrates:

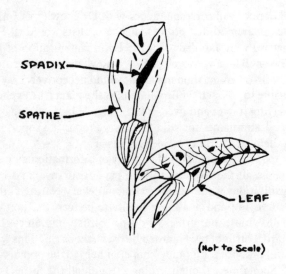

(Not to Scale)

Cuckoo-pint grows in hedgerows, woods and gardens all over the country – notice it once and then you can't miss it. It has the weird and wobbly spadix in the summer and poisonous scarlet berries in the autumn. It's a suggestive looking plant if you think about it – and generations of country folk have thought about it to judge by its endless list of popular names. Some of these names are too embarrassing to mention here, but in general the names veer from the gruesome: dead men's fingers, snake's food; to the religious (referring to the hood-like spathe): parson in the pulpit, quaker; and to the sexual (referring to the spadix): lords and ladies and cuckoo-pint. Pint is an abbreviation for penis.

The plant also has an interesting history of uses – from food (its roots were ground and made into bread and it's said Julius Caesar's army lived on this during one of his campaigns) to the component of a fiendishly effective starch, and even Parisian face powder!

We first investigated the plant in February when the dark green spears of its tightly folded leaves were pushing through the ground. Peter drew it for the magazine, telling the readers that some of the leaves would be blotched with purple when they opened and others would be plain green and adding firmly that the plant did *not* belong to the fly-eating category although this looks likely: 'The story about cuckoo-pint eating flies is not true. In fact, what happens is that the spike – or spadix – is slightly warm and attracts flies to warm their feet. When they land on it, they fall into the plant and get well dusted with pollen and fly off to fertilize another plant.'

To our surprise, readers started to respond. Children told us they had the plant growing in dark corners of their town gardens, and Staff HMI (and author of impressive texts on brain development) Dr John Brierley posted his comments to Peter and Matt:

> I was interested in Peter's account of cuckoo-pint and his observation that its leaves show differences between plant and plant. If you look carefully the leaves of different plants can not only be speckled or plain but vary in shape and lustre. It is a very variable plant. Its spathe – the spike surrounding the flower – can be dull purple or pale green. The poker-shaped spadix inside can be yellow or purple, while the spathe can be rolled clockwise or anti-clockwise!
>
> Spotting and recording these variations is important to the naturalist, but what advantage the different forms have is unknown. So look out in May!
>
> In Bristol, the percentage of plants with a purple spadix is about 70%, yellow 20% and intermediate 10% but in other parts of the country different proportions are found. The plant is called angels and devils in Somerset but bulls and cows in Derbyshire where I come from. Remember it is a poisonous plant, not just the red berries but its leaves and root. Mary Howitt, the poet, called it a 'hooded mystery'.

It was a mystery to us, too, how Julius Caesar's army survived on poisonous bread! However, that wonderful description – the 'hooded mystery' spurred on investigation and while we were planning an expedition to look at each local spadix to see if it was purple or yellow, I came across the following intriguing reference to the plant in Thomas Hardy's *Tess of the D'Urbervilles*. Tess is sitting by a river bank engaged in a sort of 'he-loves-me-he-loves-me-not' activity unpeeling cuckoo-pint to see what colour the spadix is:

> 'It is a lady again,' interrupted she, holding out the bud she had peeled. 'What?'

'I meant that there are always more ladies than lords when you come to peel them.'

Tess of the D'Urbervilles (Chapter XIX)

There was something odd about this. Botanists seem to agree that the plants with the purple spadices are 'lords' and the paler, yellow ones are 'ladies'. Yet here was Tess – admittedly 100 years ago – but in Hardy's Wessex, not that far from Bristol, complaining that she always ended up with a lady!

Now, this may have fitted Hardy's symbolism but it was enough for us to decide we had to launch a proper survey and test the Bristol variations. We'd experienced survey forms which were overloaded with questions and which, frankly, demanded too much self-discipline, so we decided to ask a minimum of questions. Keith designed a survey sheet asking readers to record the location of plants surveyed, the date, whether or not the leaf was spotted, the length of the longest leaf in cm and the colour of the spadix.

There was a setback, however. This year the plant chose to drag its feet and was not flaunting its spadices on time. We had selected a date to go out on our own special *Eye on Local Nature* team survey – but this date had to be postponed. I remember taking this very seriously and getting a headache about the plant's perversity! Meanwhile, while out in the woodlands encouraging the plants to unfold their spathes, Peter found even more mystery – the plant was under attack:

As I was out prospecting for our cuckoo-pint survey, I noticed that the spadices are late and this means we must postpone our survey for two weeks.

An interesting phenomenon was that nearly every one of the spathes we saw in some areas had been cut off. Sometimes the spadices had gone. This cannot be people as the broken ones were off the beaten track and in inaccessible places. These spathes have been cut in exactly the same place – just above the bulbous lump. Have readers any ideas? Also, on the Downs, some of the spadices which have appeared have been partially eaten – leaving what look like teeth marks. Could this be squirrels or large birds?

Reading through *The Natural History of Selborne* by Gilbert White that very same week, I discovered that this attack and nibbling of cuckoo-pint was a question which had puzzled him in the eighteenth century:

I had remarked, for years, that the root of the cuckoo-pint (arum) was frequently scratched out of the dry banks of hedges, and eaten in severe snowy weather. After observing, with some exactness, myself, and getting others to do the same, we found it was the thrush kind that searched it out. The root of the arum is remarkably warm and pungent.

Selborne, March 30, 1768

At last the plant unfolded its spathes in hundreds and we embarked on our own survey day, a fast-working, rather competitive three hours as Dr John Brierley and his wife, biologist Dr Ann Brierley, Matt and Peter, Keith and I, raced around the woods of the huge Ashton Court Estate on the outskirts of Bristol comparing the colours of the spadices.

Together with the forms from our readers, we had hundreds of spotted and plain, purple and yellow cuckoo-pints to analyse. Fortunately, Keith is a chartered accountant and could bring his statistical skills into play to make sense of the variations. Our conclusions were that 72% of the spadices were purple (and this included black and red ones!) and that 28% were yellow (and this included other pale shades, including a lovely lime green). Keith also discovered that there was a higher incidence of spotted leaves among plants with purple spadices.

I don't think there will ever be an end to the cuckoo-pint story. Readers continue to write with their observations and theories. This year's spathes are just opening – but never mind them, we've just noticed that some of the purple blotches on the leaves are very strange indeed . . .

Journey to the past

What next? This time a reader requested a survey. Producer Caroline Weaver was curious about all the wild plants growing by the side of the road and in the pavement on her route from home to the BBC. 'I mean to take my wild flower book and identify them all and write a list for you,' she wrote, 'but perhaps you and Matt could do that one evening?' Eager to prove themselves, Matt surveyed one side of the road, Peter the other and between them the boys identified and listed 74 wild plants for the rather surprised Miss Weaver!

By now, though, it was heading towards the winter. What could be surveyed in winter? We might go anyway, but would readers be likely to venture very far in the cold and wet, recording things for us? We thought not. However, the boys had a different idea. What about an indoor investigation? What about old Nature books? We had a good stock of them culled from jumble and book sales. It's still possible to get them – but I warn you that old botanical books, especially with colour plates are eagerly sought after by collectors.

A questionnaire was sent with the September issue, asking the readership:

What are the old Nature books you most treasure?
How did you come to have these books?
In what way do you find them interesting?
Please can you tell us the most amazing, interesting, inspiring or amusing fact or quotation in one or more of your books?
Are there any special botanical plates or illustrations?
How does the information or style compare with more modern Nature books?

The first response to this was alarming. A few days after receiving the magazine, one reader came to see us to say she'd realised for the first time in her life that she'd never *had* any old Nature books – and she handed back her questionnaire with a look of reproach. Things improved after this, fortunately. Children asked us how to track down old Nature books to start their own collections, and readers asked to see ours.

Then, gradually, the forms came back – mainly from adult readers telling us about their books: this idea struck gold! Dr Mark Smith of the University Botanic Garden replied:

About old Nature books, I would say my favourite is Edward Topsell's *History of Serpents*, published in 1608 and acquired by me many years back when such books were much cheaper than today. Its pictures are black and white woodcuts, some recognisable but others fanciful – such as that on the title page which depicts 'The Boas' as an immensely stout snake with a head the size of a cow's, holding a child in its jaws. Here is a section from Topsell's account of the wasp:

'(From) the stinging of vvaspes there doe proceede diuers and sundry accidents, passions and effects, as payne, disquieting, vexation, swelling, redness, heate, sweatings, disposition or will to vomit, loathing and abhorring of all thinges, exceeding thirstinesse, and now and then fainting or swounding; especially when after the manner of venomous creatures they have infected their stinges by tasting the flesh of some Serpents or by gathering their food from venomous plantes.'

I don't like wasp stings, but I think Topsell lays on the agony a bit too thick!

Robin Tanner wrote to the boys to tell them about the wonders of Sowerby:

Our greatest treasure is *English Botany* in 36 volumes, published from 1790 to 1814. The brief text is by J. E. Smith. The 2,591 etchings, all in line and painted in water-colours are by James Sowerby. Every one is extremely beautiful and astonishingly accurate. Indeed, whenever we need to identify a wild flower that is new to us, we return to Sowerby. No one has surpassed him.

I bought these books in 1938 in a second-hand bookshop in Bath for only £5! They are in their original binding, and this is considerably worn. Not a single page is missing, and none have ever been damaged by damp.

And then came the greatest excitement of this journey to the past. *The Times'* Nature Diarist, Derwent May, sent the magazine a hauntingly whimsical account of *Wild Nature's Ways*:

One of the favourite books on my shelf is *Wild Nature's Ways* by Richard Kearton, published in November 1903. Richard Kearton was a farmer who became a bird-watcher and Nature photographer; his younger brother, Cherry Kearton, also became a remarkable wildlife photographer, and went on to make many of the early cinefilms about Nature. The two brothers produced the first Nature books to be illustrated entirely by photographs.

Wild Nature's Ways is not only about birds and animals, but also about the adventures of the two brothers. They had a hide made by a butcher from 'the largest fat ox he could lay his hands on': the ox skin was stretched over a wooden framework. The camera was fixed on a little platform in the ox's breast, and the photographer stood inside with only his legs showing. The extra pair of legs did not seem to worry the birds, and Richard Kearton was soon photographing skylarks at their nest, and birds bathing in a pond. One of the charms of the book is that it is on strong, glossy paper, and has photographs set among the text on almost every page. There are photographs of Kearton holding the ox upside down on his shoulder, and also sitting on it; and there are some of the photographs he took by the pondside, including a fine one of a song thrush, called 'Substance, Shadow and Reflection', in which we see the thrush's shadow thrown on the water on one side of the stone he is perching on, and his reflection in the water on the other side.

Richard Kearton and his brother Cherry also had a hide made out of a stuffed sheep. They didn't try to get into this, but just hid the camera in it, with the lens peeping through the sheep's chest; the photographer established himself in a hide about 50 feet away, and operated the camera through a length of pneumatic tubing. Using the sheep, the brothers took splendid photographs of common sandpipers at their nest, and of wheatears, at a lonely little ghyll in the North of England.

Apart from such stories, *Wild Nature's Ways* is full of good observations of birds. Kearton watched a cock robin feeding its mate on the nest until she was so full that she refused to open her beak – upon which the cock robin gave the food to some young song thrushes in a nest nearby. The book includes photographs of a blackbird's nest in a tin can, a swallow's nest in an old shoe in a boat shed, and a man's hand stroking an eider duck as she sits on her eggs. Other curious photographs are of a patch of daisies asleep, photographed before sunrise, and the same patch of daisies awake after the sun had risen; and some primroses photographed in the first moments of the 20th Century.

The Keartons were not such scientific observers as most of us have nowadays become; but they did a wonderful job 80 years ago in showing people how Nature could be studied without shooting or collecting.'

The case of the four-headed celandine

The calendar, if not the weather, told us it would soon be spring again, and time for more investigative botany. Now what could we look into? Dr Mark Smith had told us that lesser celandines were *his* favourite wild flower and he was looking forward to seeing them again. And, thinking about these cheerful, shining yellow stars with their pretty, heart-shaped leaves, we realised that they certainly fulfilled three important conditions of a plant to be investigated. Celandines grew *everywhere*, flowered for ages and varied considerably in size and leaf markings. Also, we thought that to focus on his favourite wild flower would be a small token of our appreciation for Dr Smith's gentle encouragement of our botanical efforts. Dr Smith promptly gave us guidance and encouragement:

> Lesser celandine is a good subject for a survey because it is highly variable. It exists in two subspecies – the normal one without bulbils, and subspecies bulbifera with small whitish tubers in the axils of the leaves, which drop off and root apart from seeds. You will probably find that the bulbous subspecies differs from the other in some other respects also – possibly in size of flower, height of plant, type of habitat etc.
>
> You may also find, independently of subspecies, some considerable variation in the dark patterns on the leaves. It would indeed be worth looking out for forms with exceptionally attractive leaves, with orange flowers, with double flowers or with white flowers. Finally, there is likely to be some variation in size of plant and colour of leaf correlated with habitat, particularly with amount of shade.

We made a note to look out for all these points (having tracked down diagrams in botany books of the two types of lesser celandine), but we thought we should ask our readers to concentrate on three aspects of the plant only, to keep the survey simple to understand for the young children involved. We asked readers to record the number of petals, the colour of the back of the petals (this varies from green to purple), the details of the leaf pattern and its colour (some are plain, others blotched with either purple or pale green). Date and place were also, of course, to be indicated – and we left a column blank for any comments readers might have and anything unusual they found.

The questions were sent out on a form which we photocopied and sent out with the February issue of *Eye on Local Nature*. Then we had to settle down to a maddeningly long wait because although celandines can flower as early as January, this year they remained tight-lipped in protest against the long, cold, wet spring.

But before the spring wild flowers blossomed in 1984, Dr Mark Smith died. A man eager to share his passion for plants with others – and always ready to listen to the clumsiest theories and observations of amateur enthusiasts – Dr Smith is greatly missed. My heart ached at the tragedy whilst the country marvelled at the glorious spring which burst with shattering beauty in April and transformed the scenery in a matter of days.

Upset by Dr Smith's death, and understanding the significance of this survey, readers rallied loyally and completed forms started to come in. But, as we had previously discovered, 'scientific' investigations do not always proceed in straight lines. Forms in hand, staring at celandines, Peter and I literally stumbled upon the most exciting and bizarre tangent of this investigation.

We had an hour to spare during the half-term holiday and decided to survey some celandines near to home, in the brambles around the gates of the University Hall of Residence which opens onto the Bristol Downs. Our sheet completed, I was backing gingerly out of the briars in easy stages when I saw a real oddity. I now have a confession to make and thinking about it makes me go cold with shame. If there was such a thing as a botanical hair shirt, I would wear it, but as there isn't, a public confession will probably have the same effect. I will never do it again. I picked it.

Cradling this most peculiar of celandines, we ran home to measure, draw and photograph it and to telephone Trevor Baker with our discovery. We were shaking with excitement! Peter drew the flower for the magazine:

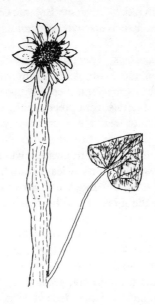

LESSER CELANDINE
(We think 3 or 4 flowers have literally joined)
Found near Wills Hall Bristol Downs
Petals: 35. Sepals: 13. Width of stem: 1.2 cm.
Depth of stem: 0.3 cm. Width of flower: 5.2 cm.
Width of stamen area: 2 cm. Height: 15 cm.
(NOTE: the flower is unable to close its petals at night.)

Dr Michael Crawley of Imperial College wrote at once, explaining that the celandine was 'fasciated', telling the magazine's readers that . . .

Fasciation is an intriguing biological phenomenon, about which experts hold differing opinions. Some argue that it is caused by somatic mutations (genetic alterations during normal non-meiotic cell divisions), while others allege that it is a consequence of infection of small wounds by bacteria like Phytomonas species. In your area, it should be possible to find fasciated individuals of sweet pea, forsythia, elder, creeping thistle, dandelion, oil seed rape and evening primrose.

Finding fasciation is a game everyone can play! Matt's younger brother Sam braved the school caretaker to get a small sample of a fasciated shrub in the school playground, Trevor brought us some fasciated forsythia, the University Botanic Garden sent some fasciated prunus – and Peter soon discovered a dandelion with a thick stem and three heads.

As for the celandines – *everything* varies! Readers and editors looked at 236 flowers – and the complexity of information returned to us was astounding. The 'average' number of petals is 8 – but this varied from 6 to 14. Backs of petals were green, pink, bronze, silver-yellow and mauve, and the buds were green, carmine, yellow and pink. The stem colours were apple-green, bronze and red – and the colouring of the leaves and presence of blotching varied widely.

Some plants with the tiniest leaves laughed at us with the largest flowers, some petals were like buttercups (rounded), others thin and pointed. Late in the survey we realised that despite what the textbooks said, many flowers had 4 sepals not 3. Was this on flowers with more petals than the 'average' 8? It looked like it – until we found an 8-petalled flower with 4 sepals! But the biggest mystery of all was: why so few red stems after March?

This was a romantic survey; readers strove to find exact descriptions for the colour of the buds, petal backs and leaves – and the loveliest of shades were chosen: 'silvery yellow', 'palest grey', 'pinky, warm brown', 'deepest brown', 'shining bronze'. Always ready to highlight the unusual, Trevor Baker commented of one plant, 'lush growth, but was in competition with a large clump of Arum maculatum (cuckoo-pint)' – and Peter and I rushed off to investigate celandines growing next to cuckoo-pint. Could they have an effect on each other? We weren't sure, until we discovered one celandine plant with leaves spotted with purple where it grew next to a spotted-leaved cuckoo-pint – and plain on the side where there was no cuckoo-pint!

I believe Dr Mark Smith would have been satisfied with our celandine survey. I'm sure, too, that he would have been pleased that the University continued to help us. Going through Dr Smith's papers – and astonished to see just how *much* he had been involved in – the Curator of the Botanic Garden, Dr David Gledhill, wrote to Peter offering his own services as consultant. So our precious link with the University Department of Botany continues – and this is why I am just about to go to the Bristol Downs to look at hawthorn buds. You see, Dr Gledhill writes his 'casebook' for *Eye on Local Nature* – and one of his recent mysteries was the *Case of the Jumping Buds* . . .

FINDING OUT MORE

☐ Those Latin names. It isn't necessary to memorise them – but it is a case of not blocking your mind to them when they are used. Most botany books use both classifications and if an expert writes to us using only Latin names, then we'll reply in kind. A warning – and I have seen this happen – never be coy about Latin names with experts in this field, remember you'll be laughing at the language of their science.

☐ Surveys are excellent to make you focus in detail on your surroundings – and once you have acquired this skill all kinds of discoveries will become possible! However, never be so intent on ticking the form that you can't get side-tracked by what else you see. The surveys of established wildlife organisations showed us the possibilities and got us started on recording and comparing – but it was our own curiosities that fuelled our progress.

☐ We increase our knowledge simply by not putting off looking things up, by not resting until we've identified a bird or plant new to us, or tracked down an explanation for an unusual aspect of its appearance or behaviour.

☐ When you discover something strange, first take all the steps you can to verify that it *is* unusual – not just a commonly occurring variation. Refer to all the books you can, contact local experts, amateur and professional. Collect all the main data – size, location etc. (take a photograph if possible) and act *quickly*. Send all your information to the nearest relevant University Department or to the head of one of the wildlife societies or organisations, asking for his or her comments on what has caused the variation, or strange behaviour. Professionals seem to enjoy the sense of urgency amateurs bring to the subject – they find this in some way endearing and always respond with information!

☐ The BBC Wildlife Unit in Bristol is very approachable – and if you don't live too far away and they have a cameraman to spare, you may find your discovery rocketed to fame! At the moment they seem especially interested in wildlife in towns and cities.

Part five
CAPTURING MIRACLES!

Every week we go on safari. I'm the hunter, the role I relish most in all our Nature adventures, and Peter and Keith follow with their cameras, lenses, extra films – and their never-to-be disappointed expectations that I'll come up with *something* rare, strange and beautiful.

And, of course, this is how I go on finding the unusual – just like all the four-leaved clovers of so many years ago. If I find a twin-headed anemone for Peter, I'll look even harder at the woodland floor and track down a six-petalled tormentil for Keith. In the spring and summer it's easier – there's almost too much to find – but in the winter responsibility weighs heavily on me. I'll follow every suggestion of a path, track every scent and produce little miracles to capture on film: cyclamen by a woodland path, violets flowering late into the autumn beside a fallen pine cone, primroses deep in the snow – months earlier than usual. Then, in the summer, while Keith and Peter photograph the abundance of wild flowers vying for their attention, I'll climb rock upon rock to track flowers which were supposed to have ceased flowering in the Gorge decades ago – and I have my own motto for these photographic safaris: if it's there, I'll find it.

Then, later, when the dozens of photographs and slides return (Keith takes slides, Peter prints – it defuses some of the competition between them), it's my job to act as editor, agent and promoter for their photographs, ruthlessly weeding out the pictures which don't do justice to the flower or their talents – and making sure that the level of appreciative outlets is kept high. Simply, I find a *use* for all these photographs and generate a need for dozens more of them – of higher and higher standard!

Obviously, photography could survive without this kind of stimulus and purpose – but I've seen how much it thrives and blossoms with them. I make sure Peter and Keith have a wide audience for their pictures. There are lots of books on the basic techniques of photography and I don't want to duplicate that guidance here. However, the actual *uses* of amateur photography, especially specialist photography of this nature are far from self-evident.

First, though, I'd like to share Keith's experiences as a wild flower photographer. Close-up flower photography is an art form – we're talking about a specialised and very wonderful form of portraiture, its subjects more beautiful and just as contrary as any human sitter:

'Just as the best human portraits are often taken with the light that's available (daylight), so are the best plant photographs taken in natural surroundings with natural lighting. You have to be a masochist to do this as an adult because not only is the process of taking the photographs in situ made difficult by the practice of many plants of growing at ground level, frequently in inaccessible and hazardous places, but the plant itself is also surrounded by natural defences such as nettles and briars. The ground, too, is invariably strewn with anti-personnel devices such as horse chestnut cases and sharp flints. It's usually both wet and muddy and uneven so that not only cannot you get comfortable as you grovel before the flower, but your thermos falls over and empties into your hat, both of which you need because it is numbingly cold. The camera slips from your fingers which have gone like cardboard because of the cold, there is a nasty wind blowing up your trouser leg, the sun has just gone in for the twentieth time (this time for good), the light level has fallen alarmingly, needing heartstoppingly long exposure times, or the tripod you didn't bring or can't afford. The wind swings round and the wretched plant starts to shake like a dervish, moving tantalisingly in and out of focus which at these close distances is rather critical; then, just as you get it all lined up and your finger trembles on the shutter release, hoarse shouts are heard from the rest of the party – those of them not in the final stages of hypothermia – to the effect that it is starting to rain. And it does. It is no good explaining to those who are cold and deprived of their hot drink through your negligence, the benefits of photographing natural subjects when they are wet (interesting highlights, increased colour saturation, tactile waterdrops) and how, if you bend over the camera it won't get wet, their thoughts are elsewhere.

As you are on the way home, miraculously, the rain stops, the sun comes out, the fields are alive with a thousand images and it is all achingly lovely. But you have now run out of film, time, patience and friends!

So why do it? If the success rate is very low due to the hit and miss nature of the technique, why bother? No wonder other people use 'flash and grab' techniques (pick the flower, and photograph it at your leisure in your nice warm studio, or, if it's protected or you have a conscience, bash it off with a flash especially a medical ring flash that leaves no shadows at all!).

If you could see Peter's photographs of the wild flowers of the Avon Gorge, you could see what it is all about. He goes through all the difficulties I have set out above – difficulties that would be enough to floor most adults (including me on occasions) and he genuinely doesn't seem to notice. He is at that first love stage with his camera where the excitement is in the taking of the picture, what he sees in the view finder at the precise moment he takes the photograph. Peter doesn't seem to doubt that every picture will be a success – and isn't at all put down when some of them fail for technical reasons like faulty exposure or camera shake. As long as we don't rub his nose in the failures, he is quite unperturbed. When Peter is working, he keeps up a monologue addressed to the subject, rather like a professional shooting a human model, 'Yes, . . . that's lovely, that's great . . . hold it there . . . '

The pictures themselves at their best, after we have done our usual editing job on them (Peter doesn't take much interest in them after they have come back) are almost human, a quality that we first noticed in a small amount of my best work on slides that we were editing into a short sound/slide sequence for a competition. Peter has this talent to a much greater degree and he isn't inhibited by received concepts of what a flower photograph should look like. He breaks all the 'rules', opens up the lens to full bore and shoots away happily. And his portraits have about them a breathtaking, almost religious awe.'

But what of the photographs themselves? What do we *do* with the hundreds of prints Peter and Keith take in a year? After Keith has matched each print to its negative, dated and numbered it, I sort through objectively and discard anything which is substandard. Photographers can be too sentimentally involved with their own work and it needs an outsider to do this. I've edited the work of professional photographers who have blenched at the speed with which I select. But a photograph has a matter of seconds to make an impact and I trust my first reactions.

From Peter's finest prints, we have formed our own botanical record of the flowers of the Avon Gorge – a rival to any textbook in its scope and accuracy. In this conservation conscious age, too, picking flowers is becoming taboo and photography is an essential tool of the botanist – close-up work especially so. I turn to Peter's records as often as to textbooks if I want to verify a scientific fact about a plant – number of petals, shape of leaves – and the exact time it was flowering in a particular year. As we are now consulted by wildlife interests, it's useful to be able to turn to the photographs to see the profusion or state of health of a flower in any particular year. Comparing this with its current state helps us to substantiate our opinion on the plant's need for protection, more shade or more light.

I use Peter's photographic records, too, as a source book for my own drawings and paintings. If I pick just one bluebell to draw, Peter's photographs can give me other angles and compositions to include. Rare flowers like orchids, angular solomon's seal and fritillaries are drawn for the magazine entirely from Peter's photographs.

Peter started to include flower photographs with his Bristol Nature Report to Mr May of *The Times*. To do this, of course, we needed to get the prints back quickly – within the week – so we were not sending him pictures of the first violet buds in the middle of June! Eventually, and shyly admitting that he was not a photographer like Peter, Mr May sent Peter one of his own efforts – of a red-necked phalarope – to accompany an article for *Eye on Local Nature* about Iceland.

Artist Robin Tanner lamented that he did not often see the wood spurge that Peter described in the magazine – and Peter took it upon himself to photograph this amazing plant in all its stages, from its early yearnings to its later geometric strangeness, to send to Mr Tanner so that he could share it.

As we now correspond with experts in the botanical and conservation field, photographs are essential for verification (and obviously, the clearer and more close-up the photograph, the more seriously we are taken). Photographs take away the element of doubt: we can prove what we saw. If, too, speed is vital – and this happens in the case of orchids – Keith arranges for same-day processing for Peter and the photographs can be on their way to one of our network of experts within 24 hours. Peter's photographs of wasp orchids have been used by the University as a teaching aid. However, Trevor Baker quickly removed them from the wall when the legendary and dreadful lady orchid collector from Kent arrived at the Botanic Garden! As payment for articles for his magazine, Peter's prints have gone all round the county and country. Many, we know, are framed and displayed.

We don't buy many Christmas presents or greetings cards. We compile portfolios of Peter's best photographs, tied with a velvet ribbon, to send as presents – sets of orchids, bluebells, spring flowers, white flowers for Robin Tanner and Mr May. Wonderful greetings cards and calendars are made by fixing the photographs onto good quality coloured paper with photomount. These also form Peter's contribution to his school's summer and Christmas fair.

It matters to me that we try to share the beauties of the Avon Gorge with people who cannot see it because they are too ill, handicapped or elderly to be sufficiently mobile. Keith had already given flower slide shows for elderly people at a local community centre and I decided that there must be similar uses for Peter's prints. We wrote to one of our largest local geriatric hospitals asking them if we could form a link between *Eye on Local Nature* and some of their patients – would they like to receive photographs of Leigh Woods and the Avon Gorge? They would – and this incidentally put us in touch with a hospital porter who told us about rare poplars and albino bees . . .

So, for a year, we sent photographs to Manor Park Hospital along with the magazine – and the hospital occupational therapists shared them with the patients and made a display of the woods in every season.

I asked Peter, who was then twelve, if he felt he could go a step further and go to the hospital with me to talk to the patients about the woods, taking more photographs with him. He agreed. The meeting was organised by the occupational therapists as a pioneering project for the hospital. No-one knew if it would work – or if any discussion or reaction at all would be forthcoming.

When we arrived, the patients were ready for us – fourteen elderly and disabled patients in wheelchairs around a huge table – and four occupational therapists.

Peter talked first about badger watching, and then about the wild orchids, flowers and birds of the Avon Gorge. He passed round some of his photographs and books – and my collection of wooden bird brooches, carefully fastening the clasp on each one so that no-one would get scratched by accident. Then one elderly lady tapped the table for silence and announced imperiously, 'I can't hear a *word* . . .'. Peter dried up, looked frightened and bit his lip – until an elderly gentleman manoeuvred his chair to him, winked and whispered, 'She's a daft bugger.'. Peter giggled and carried on for nearly an hour. Afterwards, we learned from the occupational therapists that they hadn't expected him to be able to keep their interest in Nature for more than five minutes!

After tea, Peter passed round his photographs and went with me to chat to each patient individually. This was best of all, and here the photographs came into their own. The ladies told us about the primroses and cowslips when they were young – and how the may blossom reminded them of their wedding cakes and dresses. Strangely, they all responded lovingly to the photographs of the diminutive white orchid, autumn lady's tresses – especially when Peter explained that the flower was called tresses because it was like a long, white plait braided with green. While they held one of my hands, I gently stroked the ladies' heads, showing them how much the colour of their own hair was like the tiny, silvery white flower.

One gentleman had asked if his wife could be included in the meeting although she was completely – and prematurely – senile. He had brought his own bird books in the car to show Peter. His wife could not respond to anything; her expression never changed and she did not once look towards her husband. Yet the gentleman spoke to his wife with such love and dignity – as though she were still fully with him and responding to his words. He showed her every photograph and told Peter what she was thinking about it, how, especially, she loved the dreamy pure white of the wild anemones.

Using our photographs to bring the beauty of the Avon Gorge to those who cannot see it is a preoccupation of mine. But the photographs and slides also offer me a very personal happiness. I have a sensitive record not just of the flowers we have seen – but also of how Keith and Peter see these flowers and feel about them: sometimes it is like an insight into a soul.

WILD FLOWER PHOTOGRAPHY

When you start to photograph wild flowers with dedication you will need a special camera, because most cameras will not let you get close enough to get a good picture – a clear, sharp photograph in which the subject, the flower, fills most of the picture area.

☐ There is only one camera that meets all the needs of the amateur wildlife photographer – a 35 mm single lens reflex (SLR). When you look into the viewfinder of an SLR, you look right through the taking lens (reflex viewing) and see exactly what the camera sees every time. You can change the lens at any time even part-way through a film. This means that you can do all the different types of

114

photography with one camera, buying (or borrowing!) the extra lenses you need for special jobs. Many SLR cameras set themselves ready to take the photograph, leaving you free to concentrate on taking a good picture (automatic exposure control). There are a very wide range of accessories for SLR cameras to help you deal with special situations – filters, electronic flash guns, winders, extension tubes, etc. Last but by no means least – the camera will take up to 36 shots on one loading! There is advice on buying an SLR in Appendix Two.

☐ SLR cameras are usually supplied with a 'standard' 50 mm focal length lens. This is fine for close-up (or 'macro') photography, but you do need to buy a No 2 (+2 diopter) close-up lens (cost: about £6) to screw into the front of the lens where the filters go. This will enable you to get close enough to most wild flowers to 'fill the frame' (get a big picture of the flower) and still stay 'in focus' (get sharp pictures). I usually screw a rubber lens hood (cost: about £2) onto the front of the close-up lens. It stops bits of grass and twig getting onto the lens and making it dirty, and keeps off the rain!

☐ For a beginner, whether using slide or print film, I would suggest using a 'medium speed' film – that is, one with a speed rating of 100 or 200 ASA. For very dull days or in heavily shaded conditions, consider using 400 ASA film. (The higher the ASA number, the 'faster' or more sensitive to light the film is.)

☐ Most flowers look their best in sunny conditions, but beware of white and other light-coloured flowers which will 'burn out' (look washed out) when photographed in direct sunlight because they are reflecting too much light for the film to cope with. For these, hazy sunshine or partial shadow is best. (Try shading them with your hand if there's no other shadow about.) Don't give up if the sun goes in, some flowers look superb on a dull day especially if it has been raining and the petals are wet.

☐ Wild flowers are generally very small. Get down to their level and photograph them 'side on' for effect. In practice, this often means lying down to get low enough. Take great care not to crush the surrounding foliage. Single flowers usually look better in the 'vertical format' (ie in an upright picture) so turn the camera round. You will usually need to do a little 'gardening' (removing dead grass and holding back other foliage that is in the way).

☐ The closer the camera is to the flower being photographed, the more difficult it becomes to get the whole flower sharp in the photograph. Fortunately with an SLR camera you can see this in the viewfinder. Focus the lens for maximum sharpness on the most important part of the flower – usually the stamens (centre of the flower). To get the rest of the flower reasonably sharp, adjust the aperture control ring on the lens to give a small aperture such as f8 or f11 (the larger the 'f' number, the smaller the aperture). If you have a camera with automatic exposure control, see the instruction book for the camera on how to do this. Watch that the shutter speed required for the exposure does not fall below 1/30th of a second, otherwise you may get camera shake (blur) on the photograph. Get a friend who is a photographer to explain the relationship between aperture, shutter speed and exposure! (An especially clear handbook for beginners is *Photography Exposed – an easy guide* by Paul Meighan and Bernard McWilliams, Impact Books.)

☐ Be ruthless in editing your work. When your prints/slides come back from the processors, have a sort-out session. We tear up any substandard photographs at once. It is very important to show only the best of your work.

☐ Economics of photography! Photography is an expensive activity. One of the reasons we don't run a car is because we do a lot of photography. There are ways of reducing the costs – for example, it pays to compare prices of equipment, film and processing because they vary quite widely. See Appendix Two for hints on this.

Part six
OPERATION
SCOOP

Like all friendships forged by shared commitment, the love of Nature unites, reaches up and down the generations and challenges our conventional notions of what is possible.

Operation Scoop is the story of Peter and Matt's friendship with Robin Tanner, the celebrated artist whose work inspires and speaks to us most in all the world, and with Heather, Robin's writer wife – and with their foster-son Dietrich, rescued from deportation to a nazi concentration camp. The friendship, the many-stranded way it grew – and how it influences every day of our lives is more than we could ever have hoped for. And, at a time when many of us feel the magic of childhood at risk, it is a testimony to breathtaking generosity.

Matt's mum, Maggie, started the adventure by nagging and shaming us into going to an art exhibition (I'd never actually been to one before) to see the *Robin Tanner Exhibition* at the Bristol City Museum.

'Just peep in, for goodness sake,' she urged, 'it's the kind of thing you'd like – you're always sitting around in woods.' So, combining it with a Christmas visit to get old-fashioned humbugs at the museum shop, we went.

It was amazing. Robin Tanner's etchings, his drawings and paintings of his beloved Wiltshire were a revelation. Here was an artist who not only felt but revelled in and could give form to what I was always trying to find – at first up the clump and, now, in the woods. These were powerful pictures. I wanted to be in the countryside Robin Tanner drew, to touch those cool stone walls, to walk down the paths through the woods and fields, to sit in the sun beside the flowers. The museum had produced a book by Robin Tanner to accompany the exhibition – *The Etcher's Craft*. Keith bought us this as a Christmas present – and we were able to look again and again at some of those wonderful pictures. I felt validated – it *was* all right to feel the way I did about woods; someone else, someone far more talented felt that way too – and more so! Robin Tanner became our hero and standard of excellence. But we certainly never expected him to become our friend.

Wild furry life was the next stage in this peculiar ladder of events. Peter, by now adept at plant photography, wanted to try wild furry life – but all we saw of this in the woods was rapidly shooting up trees or scuttling under dead leaves. We had to make a start with tamer wild furry life! The best source of this was Brandon Hill – a park in the centre of Bristol with squirrels so used to human company that they would sit still almost long enough to be photographed.

At first we fed them peanuts – but they jumped up on our knees and gorged these so quickly that Peter didn't have time to adjust the camera. An experienced photographer told us to give them brazils as it takes them just that bit longer to eat!

Brazils it was, then, and our Saturday morning squirrel photography sessions lasted throughout the autumn and into the early winter. It became very, very cold waiting around for the squirrels to appear and I'd even eat half the bag of brazils to keep going. By 10.30 we were ready for several cups of coffee and we'd head towards the local shops. Then, one Saturday morning in December, the National Trust opened a shop, a coffee shop, just behind Brandon Hill.

The squirrels were sold short after that because the coffee shop had rival human attractions, being run by three friendly gentlemen who greatly appealed to Peter in their combination of exaggerated good manners and hilarious incompetence over the timing of the coffee and cooking of the flapjacks. We went to the shop so often (every morning in the Christmas holidays) that Peter soon became known by name and the gentlemen began to anticipate our arrival and feign gratifying concern if we were a minute late.

Although the Trust Shop is usually packed now, it certainly wasn't then – hardly anyone knew of it. We took it upon ourselves to tell all our friends and took the shop's posters around the local libraries. An official opening day was scheduled for the shop and then – catastrophe – it snowed heavily and the crowds hoped for did not materialise. Not knowing that it was opening day, Peter and I trudged through the snow to feed the squirrels and to go to the shop as usual. The warmth of our welcome was lovely; the gentlemen assured us that *of course* we were better than the crowds they had expected. Peter's friendship with the 'Gentlemen of the National Trust Shop' was secured.

A few months after this, *Eye on Local Nature* was launched and the National Trust gentlemen displayed copies in the shop, putting them on the tables for the customers to read. By the close of the year, Keith had bought us Heather and Robin Tanner's best-seller, *Woodland Plants* – a celebration of the plants of their local woodland. This quickly became the magazine's most used botanical reference book with Heather's detailed and accessible text and Robin's lyrical drawings. The boys had started Operation Newshound and although we were unaware of it, the strands of the story were beginning to come together.

At first, the magazine produced so much work that weekends became very full and, sadly, we neglected our friendship with the National Trust Shop. Then, one especially dismal January day, we decided to renew the friendship – of the squirrels and the shop.

Eye on Local Nature was on display on the tables. Only one of the three gentlemen was there and, as it was so early in the morning (we were waiting outside the railings for the shop to be unlocked), there wasn't much demand for coffee. There was time to talk. This gentleman was an artist himself – and he had run a magazine at school. When he had been teaching art, he reflected, he encouraged his pupils to write to the artists they admired. Artists like encouraging youngsters, and they seemed to like talking about their work. The conversation changed but we were only half-listening. The beginning of an idea was forming. A lady came in for coffee and Peter and I were left alone. We looked at each other.

'Shall we have a go at writing to Robin Tanner?' Peter whispered.

'Yes,' I replied, adding less courageously, 'let's think about it anyway.' We ordered another flapjack to celebrate the idea. Operation Scoop was born.

Keith took up the challenge of locating Robin Tanner's address, finally tracking it in a Royal West of England Academy Art catalogue. Matt and Peter decided to compile a list of four questions to ask Robin Tanner and Peter wrote the accompanying letter. He explained how much use and enjoyment the boys were finding in *Woodland Plants* and what a 'scoop' it would be for the magazine if Mr Tanner would be kind enough to answer just a few questions. Much later, we learned that Peter's use of the word 'scoop' had prompted Robin Tanner to say to his family, 'We *have* to reply to this boy . . .'

Just one week after Peter's letter – an envelope written in Robin Tanner's beautiful italic script arrived. We were overwhelmed. Each question was answered with seriousness and depth – and the letter from Heather and Robin was warm and encouraging.

Overjoyed, Peter wrote back at once, telling Heather and Robin

121

Tanner that they were elected Life Honorary Subscribers to *Eye on Local Nature*, and that their answers would be the star feature of the March issue.

There was one issue before this, though, and Robin Tanner's response to the February issue of *Eye on Local Nature* was a turning point in the development of the magazine. His comments on the drawings of the cover, mild as they are, were devastating:

> Dear Peter and Matt,
>
> It was very kind of you to send us the February issue of *Eye on Local Nature*, which we greatly enjoyed reading – especially the cuckoo-pint article and your account of the walk with the Forest Warden.
>
> I must confess that I felt rather sorry for the poor little snowdrop on your cover! It has no curved sheath, no ovary, and the petals and sepals aren't clear, and the stalk looks like a thin wire! But I expect you had to draw it in a hurry – and probably from memory.
>
> With best wishes from us both,
> Robin Tanner

Mr Tanner had drawn a snowdrop on his letter to show Peter what he meant. Peter's feelings were a mixture of joy at owning an original Robin Tanner drawing – and burning humiliation at bringing the criticism upon himself. To complicate matters, the snowdrop had been drawn by Matt and, as Robin Tanner surmised, in a hurry and from memory. Peter was crestfallen. The post had arrived just before he left for school. In ten minutes, I would be late for work. Fortunately, like most mothers, I do my most creative thinking when in a tight corner with an upset child. I told Peter to go and get a magazine and we'd look at the controversial snowdrop.

There was no denying it – the flower was badly drawn – but there was no question of Peter blaming it on Matt.

'Look,' I said, 'Robin Tanner has a point. The picture isn't accurate and it lets the cover down. We'll have to learn from this and design the covers *first* in future.'

'But what do I say when I write to Robin Tanner?', asked Peter. 'Thank him,' I remember telling Peter, hoping I could come up with something before I was hopelessly late for work, 'he's taking you seriously, Peter, and that's a terrific compliment. Just tell him the truth – that the covers are always put together in a hurry at the last moment – and that now we realise it would be more professional to design the covers first.'

'I'll thank him for his picture of the snowdrop, too!' Peter said, more brightly, leaving for school and leaving me to pick up the pieces of my own equilibrium.

The March magazine starred the Tanners, the feature spreading over three pages:

HEATHER and ROBIN TANNER

Your Editors are proud to present this article because we both admire the work of Heather and Robin Tanner very much indeed and we greatly appreciate their answers to our EYE ON questions.

Have you ever tried to draw Winter Heliotrope? (See my picture Issue 13 of Eye-On) It is hard to make it look beautiful!

Yes. I have drawn it in black and white, and also in colour. Your description is quite perfect. We love this plant. We have a patch in a wild part of our garden. It is very invasive, we find.

Are there any plants you find particularly hard to draw?

Yes: mainly umbelliferous ones — such as Hogweed, Pignut, Hedge Parsley, and Hemlock — because of the difficulty of showing each individual tiny flower and, at the same time conveying the true portrait of the plant as a whole.

Is there any plant left you would like to draw?

Yes: Lady's Slipper Orchid (Cypripedium calceolus), which we have never seen growing in the wild. As you will know, there are only a few plants left in England, and it is right that they should be carefully guarded.

Which are your favourite seasons of the year?

I enjoy them all, but especially early Spring (or late Winter.) Winter is full of life if you look for it.

Is there anything else you would like to tell us, please?

We had no intention of writing a book about woodland plants. When the stocks of our book "Wiltshire
Village" and the blocks for the illustrations were
destroyed in a raid in 1940 our publishers (Collins)
asked us to write another book, but woodland plants
did not interest them. We have always been specially
fond of them, and from 1940 to 1980 I made pen
drawings of the plants as they appeared, and
Heather wrote about them. This was for our own
interest only. When the print dealer and publisher,
Robin Garton, saw the drawings and the MS. he
begged to be allowed to publish them as a book.
We tried to dissuade him because we felt sure that
very few people would buy such a book. He thought
otherwise, and he was right. The first edition
sold out within twelve days.

You may like to know that we accept no payment
at all for our work. Instead we arrange for
cheques to be paid direct to causes about which
we feel deeply — The World Disarmament Campaign,
The Woodland Trust, The Crafts Study Centre in
Bath which we helped to found, The Campaign for
Nuclear Disarmament, and Friends of the Earth.

The response to this issue from Wiltshire was immediate and warm,
and, mercifully, complimented Peter on his drawing of violets on the
magazine cover.

Then, in April, the correspondence took a delightful turn because,
when writing to thank Peter and Matt for the magazine, Robin and
Heather Tanner told the boys about their own garden at Kington
Langley, and began to detail their own Nature observations.

It was most kind of you to send us your extremely interesting Birthday
Issue of *Eye on Local Nature*. (We are wondering what will happen when
you leave your primary school.)

Your cuckoo-pint survey will be interesting. In our garden we find quite
extraordinary variations in the hood (or 'spathe'); some are long and
narrow, while others are broad and wide open. Last year I drew one that
was almost entirely dark purple and another that was a clear, unspotted
yellowish green. One was peppered with tiny dark spots, and some had just
one deep purple blotch down the centre.

This letter also told us of the 'splendid cock pheasant' who settled in
the garden at Kington Langley. Part of the letter was incorporated

Winter Aconite buds in snow

Pen and ink drawing from *Woodland Plants* by kind permission of Heather
and Robin Tanner

into *Eye on Local Nature* and observations from Mr and Mrs Tanner
became an enchanting feature of many issues – the boys wanting to
share them with as many people as they could and this being the safest
way. The actual letters were precious! Their May letter told us more
about Heather and Robin Tanner's garden and inspired a frustrat-
ingly fruitless search around Leigh Woods for moschatel:

> You go from strength to strength! Your May issue we found fascinating
> from start to finish. We admire very much your careful, accurate observa-
> tions and the way in which you enjoy humble plants as well as spectacular
> ones. The drawings of wood-sorrel, green hellebore, larch (with its
> wonderful description), and barren strawberry are all delightful. So are
> those illustrating seashore life in Cornwall.
>
> We enjoyed particularly your account of green hellebore, Peter. We have
> one quite old plant of it in our garden. How it came here we do not know,
> for ours is an ericaceous soil – and the green hellebore normally favours a
> heavy limey soil. Your description of the flower is perfect.
>
> Two tiny plants just coming into flower in our garden, which we love, are
> moschatel and woodruff. I'm afraid many people call them *weeds*, but we
> let them wander where they will – even into the vegetable garden(!) where
> they do no harm. I wish wood-sorrel liked us as much; one tiny patch in our
> little hazel copse never increases, unfortunately. I am always hoping to find
> that strange, cadaverous parasite, toothwort, under the hazels , but I must
> be patient.

This letter was followed more rapidly than usual by another – and a
very significant one:

9th May, 1983

Dear Peter & Matt,

> This note is just to tell you that we too have occasionally found damaged
> cuckoo-pints, and we have assumed that slugs were the culprits, but we
> may be wrong. Your drawings in your letter are delightful, Peter. Thank
> you very much for them. We greatly admire your careful observation;
> Gilbert White of Selborne would have given you both high praise!
>
> We hope you will find moschatel. In our garden it seems to like the
> company of woodruff, and the two together are a very nice sight.

We send our good wishes to you.
I think we must meet one day.
Heather and Robin.

Matt was told about this at once and I often overheard Peter
muttering to himself, 'We must meet one day, I think we must meet

one day . . .'. He would soak in the bath chanting these words. And this letter was special for another reason. We had heard of Gilbert White of Selborne and his famous Nature observations but to our shame we had never read the book! A copy was obtained without difficulty – apparently it's the fourth most published book in the English language! We started to read the letters written to other naturalists by this country clergyman of the 18th Century. These letters, about White's beloved village of Selborne are uninhibited in their passion for minute detail and, because they are written by a man so totally absorbed they are themselves intensely absorbing. It seemed to us, and the thought was wonderful, that Robin Tanner and Peter were corresponding about Kington Langley and Leigh Woods in such a way as to carry on the tradition of Gilbert White, two centuries later.

We were all a bit overawed by the continuance of this friendship, and wished we had more to offer in return. Unexpectedly, our chance was to come. In one of his letters to Robin Tanner, Peter drew a picture of white herb robert, a West Country peculiarity – it's deep pink everywhere else. To our amazement, Robin Tanner replied, 'You have taught us something, for we had never heard of an albino form of that charming little flower. Only one of our books mentions it. *Flora of the British Isles*, by Clapham, Tutin & Warburg, says of herb robert, 'flowers bright pink or occasionally white.' I have an absurd passion for white flowers, and I wish very much that I had seen it. I wonder if it would come true from seed?'

Now we could go a little way towards repaying Mr Tanner's generosity – and project white herb robert seed began! Pink herb robert is widespread; it's not a remarkable plant from a distance and some books indicate dislike, saying it has a strong unpleasant smell. I love the geranium, astringent scent – and I have an admiration for the flower which defies the scrubbiest of conditions to give a show of pink, sometimes all year round. But in Bristol, there's a beautiful white form of this flower growing in cracks in the pavement and in the dry-stone walls. In fact, there are even two forms of this white flower – one with red stamens in the middle and one with yellow stamens. It's a bit of a botanical confusion and we're still working on the mystery of the yellow stamen form – but our ambition at this time was to get white herb robert seeds to Robin Tanner.

Our wild flower garden had given us some experience in seed collection, but at first I couldn't make head or tail of the seeding mechanism of herb robert – and I didn't know when the seeds would be ripe.

We turned to the University Botanic Garden for advice and Dr Smith was, as always, practical and encouraging. He took our request for help seriously, went for a walk outside his Botanic Garden, found a healthy specimen of white herb robert growing on a roadside verge and marked it with a blue stick. This plant, he wrote, would be ready to seed in four weeks – and it would be sensible to sow in batches, keeping some for the following spring. Dr Smith added, 'You would be likely to get a mixture of colours, but by roguing the seedlings a pure-breeding line could be established in Mr Tanner's garden after a year or two.'

We decided to worry about the whole question of how on earth to rogue seedlings later – and, at the suggested time, we collected seeds from the marked plant. It was a fiddly business. When herb robert seeds are ready, the seed cases explode and the seeds fly out clear of the plant. However, a few get left behind in the cases – and even more get trapped in nearby spiders' webs – so these we extracted and carefully stored in stamp envelopes.

Dr Smith himself was becoming more and more fascinated in this local white variety of herb robert. He hadn't paid it much attention before. The Botanic Garden staff were dispatched to collect seeds. These they planted and developed under special conditions which force growth. Every one of the plants flowered pink – this being a frustrating throwback to the original colour! So, as this didn't work, Dr Smith sent Trevor Baker to go for a walk and mark likely specimens of white herb robert to bring into the Botanic Garden. This venture was rendered redundant when a white plant was discovered within the walls of the Garden itself! This plant was promptly transplanted in a prominent position and labelled as a Bristol speciality. Robin Tanner, meanwhile, had received his seeds, was preparing to plant them – and wrote an extra letter to the boys.

Can you imagine the thrill of reading these words:

Dear Peter & Matt,
   Would you like to visit us? If so, I wonder if next Friday, 1st July or Saturday 2nd July might suit you? If Friday, I would write to the head of your school (or telephone) to ask if you might make this visit in connection with *Eye on Local Nature* . . .

It had, we decided, to be Friday. Matt was telephoned at once, but was out playing with his go-cart. His mother, Maggie, was very excited but there was a setback because Matt was, she believed, due to take his Silver Swimming Badge on Friday. She would find Matt and phone us back. We waited impatiently, willing the telephone to ring. Maggie telephoned; Matt had already taken his Silver Swimming Award and forgotten to tell her. Friday it was – and the idea of a day off school for the event added to the honour!

The next hurdle was that there was very little time – and Mr Tanner had given us his telephone number for a reply. All my family have a dislike verging on dread of making telephone calls. I can usually escape them on the grounds that I stutter. Peter telephoned Robin Tanner and I hovered outside the door until it was over.

Peter reassured me that Robin Tanner's voice was very friendly – a little like the gentleman in the Mr Kipling cake advertisements. Mr Tanner had said that he would have a wonderful day whether it rained or shone.

The visit, then, was to take place only five days from the day we received the letter – and I longed to hear Peter and Matt tell us all about it on their return. Much has been written and broadcast about the Tanners, their work – and the beautiful overgrown paradise that is their Wiltshire home. It was hard to believe this was happening!

Sadly, though, on the Tuesday of those five days, my mother died and I left Bristol at once to return to Kent. Arrangements for the visit to the Tanners were handed over to Keith and Matt's parents. Matt came to stay overnight with Peter, and Maggie provided some home-made shortbread as a gift for Robin and Heather Tanner. Understanding how much I had wanted to hear about the trip from the boys, Keith recorded the children's account of their day as soon as they came home brimming with excitement and detail to share with him.

The children were cherished in the fullest sense of that beautiful word. I was moved beyond words by Peter's account of their walk through the woods with Heather Tanner, 'bending over me carefully dabbing my hair with anti-gnat stuff . . .'

Both now in their eighties, Robin and Heather Tanner live with their foster-son Dietrich in an enchanting, leaf-covered house designed for them by Heather's uncle as a wedding present, some fifty years ago. The boys told us that the house and garden are so lovely that they defy description, but I'll use their words because excitement had made them unusually eloquent: 'Oh, it's so beautiful – it's got ivy and beautiful trees and I like the funny front door, I think it's oak. The front door is more or less square, isn't it? They've got these ancient door locks where you kind of lift it up and it lifts the latch up. You hold it, press down on the top of the handle and the door opens. There's a beautiful fireplace and everything is so spotlessly clean there. The garden – it's just gigantic, you could get lost in it, it's got so many paths going all over the place in a honeycomb. The flowers have grown right up. We saw a shrew twice – the same one. I mean, a *real* shrew, not a dead one, and not just a flash. It was going all round my feet – it couldn't care less! Oh, it was excellent.'

Matt tells Keith, 'We went all the way round his garden. Oh, his garden is a trip – and we were allowed to walk around *on our own* and take photographs of everything.'

Just like this undreamt of freedom, so the meal, too, was entirely appropriate to small boys: 'We had dinner which was fish and chips with peas and mint. Then we had the fancy after. That was yoghurt and cream whipped together, and then Dietrich put grated chocolate in with that – and put sugar on the top. We had endless amounts of lime soda water – we had four glasses each! Robin gave us apple juice and he shook hands with us lots of times and he's ever so jolly and he can imitate voices!'

The boys had sat on the lawn in deckchairs, seen the tame robin, visited Dietrich's beehives and seen many of Robin Tanner's books as well as his printing press with all its little trays and 'gigantic mangle'. Mr Tanner showed the boys 'all his drawings and paintings and we had a long talk about his discriminating glass which he uses for detail.'

Robin Tanner had also entrusted the boys with the secret of his wife's 80th birthday present: 'He showed us the brooch he was making for Heather, for her 80th birthday; it's got to be a secret. It's one of the double-sided ones you spin round on a pivot.'

Matt and Peter had felt completely at home from the very first. On the cassette, Keith wonders whether the boys' jeans and T. shirts had been suitable for such a special occasion. Peter replies with great indignation, 'Don't be silly. Robin Tanner would have been pleased with us if we had run up to him in rags . . .'

Incredibly, there is more to the story of Operation Scoop. Since this visit, we have all met and our friendship grows. Robin and Heather continue to produce books and etchings – and Robin has been called out of retirement from the School Inspectorate to address educational conferences – to convey the special force of his own commitment, to help a troubled education service. All the Tanners continue to actively campaign for peace and for the end of nuclear weapons.

And every week a letter from Robin Tanner arrives; engaging, moving, emotional letters from a genius. A Gilbert White of the 20th Century, Robin Tanner inspires.

THE GARDEN OF OLD CHAPEL FIELD, KINGTON LANGLEY

24 JULY 1983 Our most exciting wild flower here at the moment is the uncommon, tiny, sprawling plant, the ivy-leaved bellflower (Campanula hederacea). It has appeared on a shady part of the lawn, and we have carefully mown round it. It is extremely fragile. I will draw it for you. We wonder how it came here.

2 NOVEMBER 1983 The only fungus in our garden which we have eaten is the morel (Morchella esculenta), but I can't pretend that these little brown sponges are particularly delicious. The giant puffball we think is even better than the common field mushroom, but we rarely come across one.
Thank you very much for the *Times* article about the destructive Andricus quercuscalicis which we had not seen. Our two very old oaks have borne far fewer acorns than usual this year, but I'm glad to say they all seem perfect. We will now inspect other trees in this very oaky village.

1 JANUARY 1984 We are glad you have seen your first winter heliotrope (Petasites fragrans), Peter. A rather invasive mass of this strangely beautiful plant with a heavenly scent grows near our garage, and the first flowers are just opening.

24 FEBRUARY 1984 Moschatel has strange ways; sometimes it is here in plenty, sometimes not, but as it entirely vanishes at the end of its season I fear we may sometimes – inadvertently – destroy it. This year we will keep a more careful watch in our garden.

14 APRIL 1984 First, before I forget – some good news for you: moschatel has spread amazingly in our little copse, even invading the centre of an old hartstongue fern! Has it come from seed? It is a pretty sight. One of our celandines is silvery, and quite a number have 3 petals rather longer than the others, giving the flower an almost triangular effect.

26 MAY 1984 I've just had a stroll around the dripping garden (at 6.30 am). A tiny Beatrix Potter-looking rabbit sat eating a daisy and a blade of grass near the fruit cage and hardly regarded me at all!

2 JUNE 1984 The young rabbit that was haunting our garden and considered the fruit cage his private sanctuary hasn't been seen for three days. The last time I saw him I thought he looked ill. I went up to it and touched it, and he only very slowly limped away. I fear that myxomatosis may have attacked the poor little creature.

5 JUNE 1984 We are puzzled by the little rabbit. It never moves far from the fruit cage now, and hardly moves if we step near it. It nibbles plants, but seems rather listless. We must watch it carefully.
The bees swarmed this morning, settling very high up in a hazel, but just as Dietrich went to fetch our double ladder from the garage to 'take' them, they did what we've never known them do before – they decided to return to their hive! Now all the great mass of bees are quiet again; they really are unpredictable creatures.

23 JUNE 1984 The rabbit is now full of life and adventure – too full for my liking! I have to enclose spinach, lettuces, carrots etc. in wire; otherwise he would devour the lot.

3 JULY 1984 I'm sorry to say that the rabbit *is* stricken with disease. He is nearly blind, and his head is strangely swollen, with nearly bald patches. He eats freely, and does not seem to be in pain, but he doesn't move far from the fruit cage, and he sleeps a great deal. We seem powerless to help him. At least he is safe and unmolested, but it is terrible to witness his rapid deterioration. It was so stupid to introduce myxomatosis. Man is often a thoughtless, shortsighted creature. This little rabbit cannot be more than about three or four months old, and we hope, for its sake, that it won't live much longer.

15 JULY 1984 (from Heather) We haven't seen our poor little rabbit for over 3 days now, so hope he has died quickly. Our vet neighbour, John, said he would kill it for us if we liked. But he could disappear entirely and quite quickly when aware of approach and we couldn't bear the idea of his being chased till caught (or not caught!) and therefore abandoning his quiet haven. John agreed and advised

leaving him in what we hoped was 'peace', hopping about and browsing.

25 JULY 1984 We have not seen the rabbit for a week; we have searched everywhere. I think he has sought out some dark corner and died.

5 NOVEMBER 1984 Never in our garden have we known such vibrant, brilliant colour. It is almost embarrassing! Cherries, acers and rowans have gone mad! Every day we have to cope with a tremendous leaf fall, but we do not mind because we compost every leaf. I am using 8 year-old leaf mould now, when planting a few new shrubs, and it is wonderfully black, crumbly and pleasant to smell. I am one of that minority who loves winter, and I'm already rejoicing to find winter flowers; Vibernum fragrans is one, and also that grey-coloured periwinkle difformis.

17 MAY 1985 For half a century bats have roosted in our porch and in our log store (where wrens have a nest). Every morning we have to sweep up after them, but we don't mind. We like to feel we are hosts to these very strange (and often persecuted) little creatures.

ROBIN TANNER'S BIRDS

6 APRIL 1983 Every winter a splendid cock pheasant (with usually six wives) settles in our garden, and he likes to uproot wild arums and make a meal of the base of each one. This is quite 8″ deep, but in our sandy soil he finds the uprooting easy!

19 MAY 1983 Until a few nights ago I had no idea of the volume of a cuckoo's call. It was a quarter to nine, and twilight. After a stroll in the garden, I sat on a seat under an oak tree and a cuckoo alighted about 6 feet above and began calling. The sound deafened me! It was more like 'huff-huff' than 'cuckoo' and the volume was tremendous. I counted 60 calls, and then went indoors. But the cuckoo seemed quite unaware of me and continued tolling his bell. Earlier that evening a female cuckoo made her melodious, bubbling call, which means, often, that she is going to deposit an egg.

133

27 JULY 1983 Our special pet robin is now moulting and has lost his tail. This happened last year too. He/she has introduced not only two speckled offspring but an old male blackbird to the greenhouse. In this hot weather we have breakfast there, and they enjoy their crumbs with us!

9 SEPTEMBER 1983 That was wonderful news about the partial albino robin. We have heard – though this may not be true – that the females fly far away, even as far as France, in late summer, returning in autumn. As there are several pairs here, and a number of handsome young robins, we have entirely lost count of who is who! Moulting is over, and the one who lost his tail now has a fine new one; and early this morning I heard that peculiarly beautiful sub-song (in a minor mode, and rather sad) that robins sing in autumn. Two are still quite extraordinarily friendly; if I go to gather beans they come too; if Heather hangs out wet clothes they accompany her to the clothes line, and return with her; and if Dietrich saws logs at the end of the garden, one 'helps' him, and it is difficult to avoid hitting the little creature!

1 JANUARY 1984 It is probably wrong of us to give our robins and their two special blackbird companions cheese, but they do relish it. The ripest stilton – mainly rind – is a great favourite with them.

30 JANUARY 1984 Until two years ago that uncommon and lovely little bird, the marsh tit lived here, and we have missed it sorely. Now we are rejoicing, because today two are feeding on Dietrich's peanuts, with coal, blue, and great tits and a pair of extremely handsome nuthatches. It is good to have them back. I'm afraid the cock pheasant and his six wives, who are spending the winter here, as usual, have begun to seek out cuckoo-pint roots, but there are still plenty of flourishing plants left.

12 FEBRUARY 1984 Pheasants have nipped off hundreds of our crocuses which were flat open in the sun yesterday!

8 MARCH 1984 Perhaps I told you that pheasants unearthed and devoured quite a thousand crocus corms. What is extraordinary is that they selected only the white, cream and yellow ones.
As I write I can watch a blackbird carrying mouthful after

mouthful of nesting material. Our special pet pair of robins are being secretive, but the blackbird shows us openly where she is building.

3 APRIL 1984 We hear so much about the slaughter of migrant birds that we were most relieved when chiffchaffs returned to our garden on 29th March. That was a week later than usual, but now they call all day – as though they have never left us. Now we await the coming of willow warbler and blackcap. The cuckoo used to arrive by mid April, but last year it was a fortnight late.

14 APRIL 1984 A difficult situation has arisen here: robins are carrying nesting material to a site in the open log store in our garden-house where wrens habitually build! There is great consternation and confusion!

3 MAY 1984 The blackbirds near the greenhouse have young, you'll be glad to know.

16 MAY 1984 Alas! A squirrel or a magpie stole the young blackbirds. A new nest is being built in a more sensible place, outside our pantry window.

26 MAY 1984 First let me tell you that the stricken blackbirds rebuilt immediately, and in a safer place. It is difficult now to keep count of 'our' nests. Our latest migrants – a pair of spotted flycatchers – don't seem to have settled on a nesting place yet, but they dart to and fro near our windows, in their customary area. Suddenly, the season is so full of life that we can't catch up with it.

23 JUNE 1984 I've opened my letter to tell you that the turtle dove – which used regularly to nest in our S.W. facing hedge, but has been absent for 7 or 8 years – has returned! I don't know whether it will settle in our garden, but it is lovely to hear its soft crooning purring again.

26 JUNE 1984 Alas, the turtle dove has not settled with us, but we hear the distant seductive purring from time to time in the sloping meadow across the lane.

29 AUGUST 1984 Two speckled-brown young robins have been taught by our close friends, their parents, that the greenhouse is part of their territory. Now they also venture into the outer kitchen. Their breasts are already faintly tinged with orange-red. The parent birds are moulting untidily.

3 NOVEMBER 1984 We love the song, these days, of missel thrush and song thrush; the latter starts singing before it is quite light. I expect you hear it too.

17 FEBRUARY 1985 I think none of our birds have perished (so far!) in this cold weather. Dietrich carries out extensive feeding. One clever wren squeezes under the garage door to feed on spiders, and a goldcrest haunts our depleted wood store for insects.

18 APRIL 1985 As I write, a greenfinch just outside the window is collecting spiders' webs from the ivy. A missel thrush is 'sitting hard' in her dangerously obvious nest at the top of our Cox's orange pippin apple tree.

29 APRIL 1985 Four cock blackbirds (whose nests are on our walls) hop about the lawn about a yard apart. It looks rather comic! They don't fight, but nor do they mix; I suppose each is guarding his territory.

I think we've told you that the missel thrush's nest is placed conspicuously at the top of an apple tree. The hen's tail shows up plainly, sticking out beyond the nest. The male thrush attacks magpies when they come near. If only they would choose a secret spot to build in.

We have been ravaged by bullfinches. Every apple tree and most of the cherries have been stripped of their flower buds. What is so strange is that the birds don't appear to *eat* the buds; I've watched them nip them off and throw them down. If I clap my hands in an effort to deter them they evidently think I am applauding them, for they continue their destruction vigorously, heeding me not at all!

THE ARTIST

6 JULY 1983 I'm glad 'Wren and Primroses' gives you pleasure. It is the

smallest of my etchings, yet it is the favourite of many people. There is an impression of it in the permanent collection in Bristol City Art Gallery.

26 AUGUST 1983 Cornus kousa and a number of other shrubs in our garden came from John Scott's nursery at Merriott, when I used to do drawings for their catalogues. They paid me no money for these, and I paid them no money for the plants I ordered! We carried on a happy bartering, and we never quarrelled! I happened to find one of the old catalogues yesterday, and it occurred to me that although the plants are all garden varieties, you might be amused to have it.

6 SEPTEMBER 1983 I enclose 10 prints for the Taylor family. I used to buy these, some 45 years ago, for only a few pence each in George's Bookshop in Park Street. I hated to think that old and precious books had been dismembered, though I must confess I was glad to be able to amass a collection of pages so cheaply. You will see that 2 of these prints are by the incomparable Sowerby.

9 SEPTEMBER 1983 I am so glad the old flower prints please you. They always make me feel rather ashamed, for those early draughtsmen had superb standards.

21 NOVEMBER 1983 I have just come across a very battered copy of a King Penguin book, *Flowers of the Meadow*, for which I did the dust cover and illustrations, for our friend Geoffrey Grigson – many years ago. As you can see, it cost 3 shillings when it was published!, but as King Penguins were not often reprinted they are now so rare that ridiculous prices are charged for them. I gave this copy to one of my brothers, now long dead.
I apologise for the buckled pages, which you might be able to straighten by damping and pressing them under a pile of books.

30 JANUARY 1984 I am designing an etching to celebrate the month of April – very white blackthorn blossom against a showery landscape, spanned by a double rainbow.

24 FEBRUARY 1984 I am delighted, Keith, that my great hero, William Morris, means much to you. I owe more to that 'super-man' than to any other and his philosophy and all he stood for are immensely

appropriate for today.

Yes: the 'April' etching and 'October', which I've just finished designing, will leave only July to complete the twelve months. Actually, I have made a design for July, which Dietrich likes very much but which doesn't satisfy me. I must try again!

8 MARCH 1984 In July, Heather and I have to address an American audience on William Morris (at Gonville and Caius College, Cambridge) at which she will wear a dress printed in W.M.'s lovely design, 'Powdered Flowers', in the original Merton Abbey printing. You must see it when you visit us.

14 APRIL 1984 We haven't been able to reach the Morris Exhibition yet (at the *Institute of Contemporary Arts* in London). Several friends have mentioned a letter of mine (on display at the exhibition) to Ray Watkinson. He wrote to me a year ago about the proposed exhibition, urging me to identify the flowers on which Morris based particular designs. I pointed out the impossibility of this. Morris was an artist, not a botanist; so when designing he very properly took liberties with plants, to suit himself. Only 'Blackthorn' and to a lesser extent, 'Powdered Flowers' stand up to this sort of analysis. R.W. never replied!

25 JULY 1984 During this hot spell I have needled all day long at my 3 new etching plates, and they are now ready for biting, but I shall wait for cooler weather for that not very pleasant business, with its fumes of chlorine.

4 AUGUST 1984 Our United States friends at our Cambridge lectures were marvellous to us. I put up a display of great original weaving, block printing, drawing and printing by Morris, and Heather wore two Morris garments (changing halfway through the session). She looked as if she had just stepped out of the 19th Century. The audience gasped!

Next time we meet I must show you a sequence of drawings of the alarming stinkhorn (Phallus impudicus) which I made long ago. Surely it is the strangest of all fungi.

5 NOVEMBER 1984 Now today I am starting the long, tricky job of biting my new etchings – 'January', 'April', 'October' and

'Aldelmsburgh' (founded on Malmesbury). I detest the chlorine gas which the acid gives off when warmed, but I have the windows that face the copse wide open, so no harm is done. And a robin and a wren entertain me with delicious song from the copse!

ROBIN TANNER: CAMPAIGNER FOR PEACE

30 JANUARY 1985 Alas! Peter and Matt are growing up in a world which could be annihilated within an hour. We are now an occupied country, with 150 US nuclear bases poised to attack a hatched-up enemy!

We who care about wildlife and conservation, who deplore the wanton destruction of our landscape and of traditional agriculture in order to establish a greedy monoculture, who are shocked at the nuclear poisoning of the Irish Sea and much of our land, are still a minority, but we take heart because it is swelling. For 25 years we have struggled, in the face of appalling opposition, to make known the truth about nuclear weapons and to expose the lunacy of the arms race that is stealing all our money; and at last CND has become a voice of truth that the Government has to listen to, and our numbers are rapidly swelling.

FINALE – FROM HEATHER

20 JUNE 1985 Robin has asked me to describe the difference between blackcap and nightingale song for you, Peter. I'll try. The blackcap's song is sweet and fluty, best mimicked by a whistle. (To my dismay I find one loses the capacity to whistle in old age – does one's *tongue* grow old? I used to be good at it.) It hasn't many themes, and the basic one, described musically, is a fourth, in 6/8 time. In tonic solfa:

$$d' \mid t - d' : s - d' \mid t - d' : s - d' \mid$$

or in staff notation:

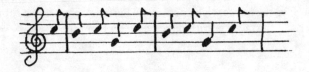

The quality is rather like a blackbird's.

But the nightingale's has infinite variety. It warbles liquidly, as if under water; but if often starts with three or four quite longish notes in the same pitch:

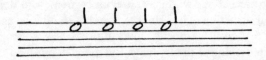

(I've chosen the key of C, but of course the birds sing much higher than this.)

A garden warbler's song approaches the same quality, but it gabbles on and on, whereas the nightingale pauses occasionally to change theme, as if in sentences. It often sings in the day as well as beginning to tune up at dusk. The last I heard – two close together – was at Greenham Common, just above the coaches, about 4 pm.

Part seven

IN CHARGE

The Avon Gorge National Nature Reserve and the Forestry Commission forest form part of one side of the River Avon: the city of Bristol sits upon the other. At the nearest point, Leigh Woods and the Nature Reserve are a mere $1\frac{1}{2}$ miles (3 km) from the city centre. The deep George forces woods and city apart and the slender Clifton Suspension Bridge connects them. To many families, as once to us, the other side of the bridge is a foreign country, wooded, mysterious, dark. A country to be stared at uneasily across the river from the cliff tops at the edge of our city.

Since our meeting with the Voluntary Warden in the woods, I had wanted to join the wardening team. We knew the woods and felt as protective of them as of our clump. It is hard to be objective about commitment, but part of it is that it's good to have a purpose and to be useful. Keith and Peter were wild flower photographers – I wanted to be a Wood Warden. So, when I raised the subject, did Keith and Peter.

I wrote to the Nature Conservancy Council Headquarters, explaining our wish and experience. My letter was treated as an application and passed to the Chief Warden of the South West Region, who replied encouragingly:

> Your offer of assistance with the wardening of the Avon Gorge Reserve is most welcome. The duties we ask of Voluntary Wardens are mostly those associated with the visiting public, patrolling, the provision of advice, preventing undesirable activities and keeping the area free from litter. However, we particularly welcome those who are prepared to undertake some physical work or who are interested in assisting with the scientific recording programme on the Reserve. All in all, it seems that your family could be ideal candidates.

Two formalities remained: an official trip around the area we would be patrolling with the Resident Warden for Leigh Woods and the Avon Gorge Reserve – and a six-month probationary period during which we were to prove ourselves worthy.

Our official meeting and tour with Michael, our Resident NCC Warden, was not promising. Newly appointed to the Avon Gorge Reserve and yet to fall under its spell, Michael was disbelieving of our enthusiasm for the woods. We were silenced, responding only when necessary to his questions about the terrain. We were to contrast two areas – the neatly cleared part of the NCC Reserve and the wonderfully alluring wilderness of the adjoining Forestry Commission forest – over which the NCC has no jurisdiction. We were to explain why some tree trunks are left where they fall – and why sycamore trees are thinned out. Our ignorance was exposed and we wondered if we had anything to offer after all. Michael outlined our duties to us. We were to remove all dangers to the public, stop horse-riders, motorcyclists and cyclists, prevent dogs crashing through the undergrowth when birds are nesting, ask campers to move, stop fires, deter vagrants, report vandalism and suspicious happenings, take part in working parties – and above all, know the woods. My spirits lifted at this last duty. We did know the woods!

And so, through the coldest, wettest, windiest six months of the year, we served our probation. Full Voluntary Wardens now, I think this preliminary period was the hardest because we had to prove ourselves both to ourselves and to the NCC without the authority of appointed wardenship to back up the actions we took. Yet how thin the list of duties seems when compared with what really happened!

Nothing in that list prepared me for my most nerve-wracking ordeal: five hours marriage guidance in the middle of the woods in a situation so desperate that even Thomas Hardy's publishers would have got cold feet about it. Nothing prepared me for how I would despise myself for finding and dismantling a vagrant's well-hidden shelter – or for how difficult it would be to persuade a young rape victim that the woods were not full of dangers, and to take her with me, step by step, to see. Nothing could have prepared me for my impotent anger when confronted by 600 orienteers using a badger sett as a checkpoint – and for the ups and downs of the campaigns which followed.

But nothing on that list of duties describes the most wonderful of times – the discovery and guarding of rare plants, the new to me exhilaration of climbing high above the Avon to take on the dare-devil graffiti painters at their own game – and the tenderness of watching badger breath rise in a shaft of sunlight from a badger sett on a frosty day and knowing we have come to protect.

While Peter and Keith are locked in the private world of photography, I explore, search – and scribble in my notebook. Because what their pictures are to them, my wardening journal is to me.

6 NOVEMBER 1983 Our first day as probationer Wardens. Cycling to the woods, I realise we have forgotten to bring a plastic bag for rubbish collection. I stop at a newsagent to buy a bright red plastic carrier bag and I am to regret this responsible act.

Entering the woods, I make a cheerful start by picking up a MARS wrapper and popping it into my carrier. But now – right in the middle of the path (I cannot pretend not to see it) there is a large lump of baby pink toilet paper. I think it may be used toilet paper. Keith's brave act is to lift it up with a stick and dump it in my red carrier. My misery is the remainder of our rounds – on this beautiful, mellow autumn morning, accompanied by the increasingly smelly (it is getting warmer all the time, you see) contents of the wretched plastic bag. I ram some dead leaves over what's in there, but just knowing it is there is bad enough – and there are few flowers to distract me. Today our total haul is two beer cans, a lemonade bottle, a Belisha beacon, two pages of a dubious magazine (shoved quickly into the bag before Peter sees them) and a sign saying MEDICS MARATHON THIS WAY. Someone has painted *Emma B was here* in huge letters on the rocks by the Avon.

A kestrel circles above us and we name a part of the Reserve Kestrel Corner for future reference. We climb from the bottom of the Gorge to the top (a constant preoccupation of ours and of most visitors to the Avon Gorge) and come out on the wrong side of the barbed wire designed to keep the public away from the dangerous cliff faces. Fortunately no one sees us.

13 NOVEMBER 1983 How can the weather change so much in a week? I am so cold I am going to die. We have started the day with a row. I have dressed in a hurry and am wearing white nylon socks under my climbing boots and I have forgotten my woolly hat. Our rubbish collection having been so fulfilling last week, Keith has brought a big black dustbin bag and it is his turn to hump it around. Spurred by the MEDICS MARATHON sign last week, Peter is concentrating hard on litter, wanting to find something even more interesting. Two paper hankies, 12 toffee papers and a ticket for the Bristol Hippodrome rattle around inside our voluminous bag.

This is not a good haul.

I can wait no longer for tea and food. We stop on a path I love – although I think I love it more when it is warm. The path winds through yew trees and round mysterious dark hollows and, because I find the darkness alluring, I wander away from Keith and Peter to explore. Oh God. Why do dark hollows always have something nasty in them? First, a huge discoloured plastic sheet, pinned to the ground by a log. Then a trail of beer cans and Evostick – and now a brilliantly disguised bivouac. I call Keith and Peter and we silently look at it and at each other. We doggedly begin to pick up the cans and the sordid putty-coloured rags and coverings. Peter recoils and I tell him to pick up the bottles and the glass. We want to be Wardens and shoving a tramp's home into a dustbin bag is part of the job. I hate myself.

20 NOVEMBER 1983 All Wardens summoned: Wardens workcamp. We are to clear part of the Iron Age Hill Fort of Stokeleigh Camp. The impressive slopes of the Camp have become covered with brambles and almost impenetrable scrub. This Iron Age Hill Fort is one of the most important historical attractions of the Avon Gorge Reserve.

We are to spend from 10 am to 4 pm cutting down the brambles and Keith has left half our food supply on the kitchen table. It has become our habit to visit Mr Bussell on arrival in the wood, to catch up on wood gossip and to see the albino robin. Whitey is feeding on rabbit corn. Mrs Bussell promises us she will bring cakes to us later on.

I am becoming obsessed with food. It is surprisingly mild. Peter, Keith and I slash away at nettles and brambles. My gardening gloves are ridiculously inadequate. By mid-afternoon, my hands are losing strength and I'm hacking ineffectually at anything above 3′. Peter keeps returning to our rucksack, ostensibly to check the sharpness of his cutting tools, actually to raid my bag of mint toffees.

The beautiful day is bringing out the sightseers: we have attracted a gratifyingly large audience. Faint with hunger, I concentrate on the snatches of conversation of the passers-by. Two men, striding, '*I'm* not frightened of going up North to University. My brother did it and he came back alive . . .'. Two confidential, Jane Austen ladies dipping and huddling through the undergrowth, 'Well, it's *difficult* if you don't admire *or* respect him . . .'

We return home, hands torn, a splinter in my knee (jeans are no defence against brambles) and I make supper out of the food Keith left on the kitchen table.

4 DECEMBER 1983 Hot air balloons are rising over the Gorge and the mists are low over Bristol as I cycle over the suspension bridge. Keith and Peter have gone ahead on the motorbike. This is the most beautiful place in the world.

The mild weather is bringing out the litter leavers again. Keith locates 2 blue plastic cups under a hazel bush and tells us they are in mint condition. He wants to keep them. Peter and I veto this. Three lemonade bottles, a Fairy Liquid bottle, a Jif lemon container – what's been going on? Sheets of revolting wet polythene. A shoe.

I will stop listing the haul of litter. One could become obsessed.

But what a morning! There's ice on the pathways of Nightingale Valley – the main route from the top of the Reserve to the Gorge below. And yet down in the Gorge it's as hot as summer on the rocks.

From the colour of their dung pits, the badgers have been feasting on yew berries.

18 DECEMBER 1983 Cold, bitter cold. Awful headwinds. I arrive at the woods in a bad temper. Keith and Peter are already there. My depression lifts when I see the pale pink buds of winter heliotrope by Mr Bussell's drain – and the swathes of mauve Christmas tinsel blown high up into an oak. Revellers, explains Joe Bussell.

The gales have blown down tree branches, trunks – and whole, ancient trees. We heave the lighter branches away from the paths and map those we cannot move to report to the Resident Warden at the end of our rounds. We are saying little to each other now because it's raining and now we are cold *and* wet. The wind is so sharp it is giving us earache. As usual, I am not wearing enough clothes. As I unlock my bike and Keith and Peter put their helmets on, we meet four youngsters heading into the woods with a formidable battery of weapons – a scythe, an axe and two saws. Keith explains kindly that wood cutting is not allowed. The youngsters are apologetic and co-operative. They leave in a battered van. They look to me like four very cold students. I remember being a cold student.

When I arrive home, Keith is reading his Survival Aids catalogue and tells me he is going to get me weatherproof gear.

25 DECEMBER 1983 I am wearing my new ugly weather outfit. Balloon-like over-trousers and matching windproof anorak. Heavy rain; foul headwinds. My woolly scarf drips icy water and sprays droplets every time I re-wind it round my neck.

We creep up behind the bush at Mr Bussell's cottage. We have come to sing carols to Joe and his wife and to prove to the NCC that we are dedicated. We start to sing *Away In A Manger* but Peter cannot sing for laughing. The carol sheet is disintegrating. The albino robin flips down from the roof of the cottage and starts to sing, perched in front of us, on the fence. The Bussells open the door. No one has come into the wood to sing carols for decades, Joe tells us – not since the Salvation Army. There is a wonderful smell of turkey from the kitchen. Joe Bussell sees the albino robin and whistles to him. The robin listens intently, head on one side and then replies.

There is no litter today and the woods are completely empty.

15 JANUARY 1984 Snow. It is impossible to cycle to the woods, and unwise to use the motorbike. The winds are heading to blizzard proportions. But think of all those animal tracks in the snow . . .

We decide to walk. It's only $3\frac{1}{2}$ miles to the Reserve. Keith and Peter leave their pyjamas on under their clothes and I pack extra food.

On arrival at the woods, we meet our Resident Warden, mending tools. He asks Keith to call him Michael, as I do, and not to be so formal. I explain that Keith isn't being unfriendly. He's been calling my father Mr Smith since we got married fifteen years ago.

But the snow is melting! People with dogs are heading into the woods and this will make identifying badger tracks more difficult. We run to the badger sett deep in the forest. The badger setts are not on the Reserve – they are in the Forestry Commission land and it takes us some time to reach them. The trees are indescribably lovely – sun shining through them and little rainbows reflecting on the melting snow.

At the badger sett there are paw prints leading into many of the larger holes and leading out again, radiating off between the trees along those little badger paths. Keith and Peter photograph the tracks. The sky darkens for more snow and an owl hoots twice. Tree branches knock together like old bones. I explore. Here, beyond our sett – four more scratching trees, deeply gored – and a communal dung pit, promise of another badger community! I could stay here forever. We follow badger paths and talk of their night-time activity.

Our ankles hurting, we trudge home and stop half-way to finish the coffee. We sit in the clump where we first met a robin so many years ago. There's a wonderful smell – it's the leaves of the sweet violets. You can smell them just once and then, for minutes afterwards, your sense of smell is muffled. I dig in the snow to look for buds and find them, tightly packed – waiting.

19 FEBRUARY 1984 How can it be so cold in Britain? We have been kept awake until 3.15 am this morning by a student party further down the road, and we are all in a bad temper. It is impossible to go to the woods. We have a row about not having a car. Why can't we be like *normal* people, I rage. There is amazement from Keith and Peter. Keith telephones for a taxi which arrives too early, while I'm searching for my woolly hat.

Joe Bussell tells us proudly that the birds on his bird-table have eaten 4 lb of nuts this week and that Whitey, the albino robin has eaten a sultana from his hand.

Powdery snow falls on us and it is even colder in the valley walk down to the Avon Gorge. My feet are painful with cold and I've lost my little toes. Dammit. At the bottom of the valley there is a huge pile of rubbish. It looks as if someone has emptied their kitchen dustbin. There's even a couple of old brooms – and, worse, the spread-around shattered remains of a dozen or so cider bottles. It's my turn for rubbish but Keith gallantly carts the heavy black bag around for the rest of the morning until the glass starts to tear through the plastic and dig into him. We find a way to carry the bag between us.

We walk through the railway tunnel at the bottom of the Gorge and sit far too long at the bottom of the valley because we now have to run back up the Gorge for the taxi home. We pass one of our badger setts and divert to look. The badgers have pulled down and chewed the thick lianas of the wild clematis and some have been dragged part-way down their setts – presumably for bedding? Rifle shots shatter the silence of the dark woodland – the police are using the firing range this morning. They have the use of one of the quarries in the Avon Gorge.

We rush through the woods and I stop because I have detected a new fragrance. Keith and Peter are exasperated. I leave the main path and discover a huge, fragrant and glorious clump of primroses wide open in a sea of gold beech leaves.

Keith does a barmy dance to keep warm while waiting for the taxi. The driver is sullen. He hates crossing the Clifton Suspension Bridge and says Brunel would turn in his grave if he could see what his bridge is like now. I fail to see what is wrong with it except that the taxi driver has to wait behind other cars to cross over. Also, Brunel never actually saw his bridge completed in the first place. I point this out. Keith flinches. The taxi driver settles his head sulkily on his shoulders and complains about women drivers.

18 MARCH 1984 Our Resident Warden tell us, gloomily, that the rock graffiti painters have started again. There's a big silly face on one of the high rocks. The face looks like Prince Charles. He refuses our offer of help to paint it out. It is, he says, dismissively, far too dangerous.

1 APRIL 1984 Joe Bussell shows us where his blackbirds have mated. 'Here, on this post . . .' It is bitterly, acutely cold. Peter is in France and I find spurge laurel for Keith to photograph. Ice is forming on my eye-lashes – and I discover that Keith has loaded his camera with a 36-exposure film – not a 20. He will stay until it is finished. I find I have the strength to engineer a row. Keith finishes his film.

8 APRIL 1984 I am in a paradise of primroses! This is a path new to us – a badger path and it is lined with intriguing snuffle holes (where badgers snuffle to get at roots). We are near the Reserve, but we are now on Forestry Commission land, and it is a strange mixture of beech and pine. And now I find another badger sett – the largest yet – with piles of limestone slabs excavated by the badgers and the sett itself is, classically, among elder trees. And here, by the sett, someone has been living with the badgers! There's an old boot, a kettle, socks – and an elaborate half-shed, half shelter. We have no

authority over this land and so are not charged with the duty of removing the shed and putting it in our dustbin bag.

We eat in a hollow behind the crossing of paths, back on the Nature Reserve. Mr Bussell walks past, noiselessly, alert, part of the woods – out of another century.

The weather is not a force at all today.

24 APRIL 1984 I'm so *hot*. All the spring flowers are blossoming at once. Mr Bussell's cottage smells of hyacinths and washing. I compliment him on his garden and he tells me there are four dogs and three cats buried under it.

Peter and Keith are lost in photography, changing lenses and films fast. Wood-sorrel, anemones (like alpine stars this year), violets, wood spurge, primroses . . .

And butterflies. I'm surveying for the Bristol Museum and count 22 peacocks and 14 brimstones in an hour, around the goat willow. I am wearing far too many clothes.

28 APRIL 1984 Joe Bussell has just heard the cuckoo! So has retired Ranger and fellow 80-year old Cecil Baker who is fiercely cutting logs at the back of his cottage. Forty years a Ranger in Leigh Woods, Cecil has retired to one of the Rangers' cottages in the woods, next door to the current Warden. Cecil is a bird man: he remembers when peregrine falcons ruled the Gorge. He rams his axe in a log and takes us to a greater spotted woodpecker's nest behind his cottage. We hear knocking and on cue, the bird's head pokes out of a birch tree like a cuckoo clock on the hour. Cecil explains that the bird is enlarging the cavity and points to all the wood chippings on the woodland path.

I like Cecil Baker very much. He's an attractive, elderly gentleman who looks like everyone's ideal grandfather. Like Joe Bussell, he's also tough, brave and nobody's fool.

In the darkness of the forest we find lily of the valley leaves and then, back out in the sunlight, cherry blossom rains on us like a blessing.

Our Warden asks us if we have heard of the badger sett by the cowslip because one of the elderly local people referred to it. What a wonderful name! Next week we will look for it.

5 MAY 1984 In one week spring has turned to summer and the trees are

in leaf. Woodland navigation is more difficult: visitors are getting lost and asking us the way out. Today I have not come to help visitors. I've come to find the badger sett by the cowslip. This has to be in an area new to us. We leave the Reserve and enter the Forestry Commission forest, on into oceans of bluebells. Cowslips do not often grow deep in dark woodland – so I am looking for glades and areas of light. And here, by a field, on the edge of the woods is a badger sett we have not see before. The holes are so large we could get down them up to our waists! We record the sett, the holes, the dung pits and the scratchings. There are, however, no cowslips here.

Come back a different way, I urge Keith and Peter, try just one more path. And it is now, a few feet along a little badger path radiating from this new sett, that we see one solitary, tender yellow cowslip. This is the badger sett by the cowslip. Keith says I am a witch.

13 MAY 1984 Joe Bussell says that the badger sett by the cowslip has been in the woods ever since he has – and there was a field of cowslips there when he was young, hundreds and hundreds, yellow as far as you could see.

Cecil Baker asks us if we know about the batcave in the woods? Peter is excited and this is enough for Cecil. 'I'll take you!' he exclaims, striding off. Cecil has already had one stroke and does daily battle with angina – but he is also unstoppable. He has not been to the batcave since the war. But now he will find it for us. It's somewhere down the side of the Avon Gorge, near a hornbeam, he thinks.

Redder and redder in the face with determination, Cecil leads us over brambles, through bushes and down the hazardous Gorge side. We have to stop this. I tell Cecil it doesn't *matter* if he can't find the cave. Cecil replies brusquely that it does to him. I cross my fingers tightly and whisper a message to God who rapidly intervenes. Keith suddenly sees a gap in the ground. Peter climbs over to it and down into it, wary of bats. The bats which used to live there have long gone and the cave is full of ancient tins. Peter laughs and heaves up a kettle, tea caddies and rusty biscuit tins.

'I used it as a dump during the war,' Cecil explains bashfully.

20 MAY 1984 Peter is on a school trip and Keith and I warden alone. It is

still bluebell time. Joe Bussell tells us that many years ago, two Sisters of Mercy knocked on the door of his cottage and wanted to take blind people round the wood. Joe had told them where to find bluebells and said to the party that the woods looked a picture at the moment. Then, he told us, he wanted to bite his tongue off because the blind people couldn't see the bluebells. But the Sisters of Mercy had assured him that yes, they would see them, in their way.

At the bottom of the Gorge, goat willow seeds fall like warm golden snow, caught in the crevices of every cobweb and rock. They even settle in our cups of tea. I stroke the leaves of columbine and feel them soft like the top of a baby's head. Lily of the valley is in flower. Keith attaches himself to a rope to photograph the flowers, hanging almost upside down on the edge of the rocks. There are many leaves – huge green butterflies – but few plants have flowered. The bottom bell opens first, and the flowers are surprisingly creamy at this stage.

Early purple orchids tower over the bluebells – I think these are rather lurid. We hear the cuckoo! First the cuckoo – then, far off, from the city, the church bells. After the church bells – a Strauss Waltz! On the other side of the river, miles away, there is a sponsored fun-run and the wind is bringing waves of amplified music to us. We put down our rucksacks and binoculars and waltz, in the darkness of the woods.

14 MAY 1984   Our probation is over – and we have passed! Sadly, we now discover that Peter is too young to be an official Warden. Is there an unofficial title he could have? No there is not. We will give him one ourselves. Peter does not appear to be upset.

23 MAY 1984   Warrant cards and military-style armbands arrive. The armbands are embarrassingly impressive, stating 'WARDEN: Nature Conservancy Council'. I put one on my arm, over my coat. It is so big it falls down again and I have to fix it with a pin.

28 MAY 1984   This is an evil, wet, Whitsun Bank Holiday. Not believing this, families struggle past us down the valley to the Gorge, wearing flimsy sandals. At the bottom of the Gorge we meet a cuddling young couple who ask us if they can climb out of the Gorge up the sides. Keith advises them to walk back the way they came. They decide to press on. Keith shrugs.

Back up in the wood, an hour or so later, we meet the same young couple still struggling to find a way out. She is walking in the middle of the path in at least six inches of oozing mud. Her legwarmers and high-heeled shoes are no longer white. They ask the way again. While Keith tells the man how to escape from the wood, I have a word with the girl. I explain that by carefully straddling the path, or walking to one side, clinging to the trees, you can actually avoid the worst of the mud. Her boyfriend stops talking to Keith and says to me, 'We had *that* row a mile back.' Slopping through the mud, they press on, punishing themselves.

1 JUNE 1984 This heat is unbearable and I have forgotten my bush hat. Joe Bussell says that Whitey, the albino robin, has three babies because she always takes four bits of cake from the table.

The fly orchids are out in abundance in the Avon Gorge – little rubies and amethysts on wands! Peter is laying on his back taking photographs and crooning a love song to the orchids. Keith and I are silent; both of us sense that we are not alone. Somebody is hiding from us. We motion Peter to join us in hiding, too, and not to give away the whereabouts of the orchids. Now we are hiding. They are hiding. Why are we hiding? I stand up. A young woman with a notebook stands up. We pretend none of us was hiding. She is very beautiful and her name, appropriately, is Rosie. Keith preens. Another girl joins her, a bearer with an Olympus camera and a heavy tripod. I make sure the girls can see my armband and ask them what they are looking for. They are in search of fly orchids and they work for the Bristol Museum Records Department. They can be trusted: horsetrading begins. We show them fly orchids and they take us to the very much rarer angular solomon's seal, close by. It is wonderful – like large lily of the valley but a more delicate apple green, and the white flowers hanging down like snowdrops. Peter is cursing because he has run out of film. Rosie now offers us little robin – which again, is very rare – in exchange for columbine. We are getting the best out of this trade. Trevor Baker has told us that this is how much botanical location is done, but he warned us that not all botanists play fair. There's a lot of skullduggery about – some botanists give misleading information or draw inaccurate maps in order to get what they want without revealing their own secrets.

As we walk along the Gorge, a grass snake rears and gives us its full demented, rustling display, waving its head to and fro and hissing. This is meant to frighten us away.

The badger setts are very smelly today: we sit elsewhere to eat our sandwiches.

2 JUNE 1984 I'm alone today. I have to see the orchids one more time. And so I do because many of them are in the hands of a plump teenager who has arranged common spotted orchids and two fly orchids like a wedding posy.

I ignore the fly orchids as I do not want to draw attention to their rarity – but I explain that the beautiful pink flowers are orchids and should not be picked. She looks at me silently beneath her long chestnut fringe, mutters she's sorry and hands the posy out for me to take. This is awkward. I refuse, explaining she might as well keep them *now* – she can't put them back. She accepts and walks on. On my way home I find the orchids have been placed carefully by the side of the path, their stems in a puddle.

16 JUNE 1984 The police have been combing the woods all week. A woman is missing, last seen in the woods near the cliff edge. Joe Bussell says that it is a rum do and suspects that it is a ruse to divert searchers while she has run away from home with a fancy man. I tell him he has a cynical view of women and am somehow inveigled into promising to give him a kiss at Christmas.

Robin Hood is being filmed in Leigh Woods and actors huddle together in a hollow which represents Robin's hideout. Peasant girls toss their shining heads arrogantly. One is wearing a gold watch.

A young film-maker on the Avon Gorge towpath is looking for herons and kestrels. Peter shows him where the kestrels live but we are stumped for herons.

We do not find the body of a woman. Perhaps Joe is right.

7 JULY 1984 Keith and I warden alone and the heat is relentless. We stay in the shade of the wood. The paths are wet from overnight rain and we move soundlessly into the darkest part of the forest. The rain has not been able to penetrate the leaves and while the paths are wet, the woodland floor is dry and rustling. Keith stops to relieve himself and I walk on down the path. There is a noise like a boulder crashing through the wood. I stand still. The boulder

stands still. A badger and I look at each other, yards apart. I quiver with excitement and am torn between keeping still to observe and motioning to Keith to see the animal. The badger turns and walks deeper into the forest.

12 AUGUST 1984 Today we are taking a party of 37 adults and children around the woods to see the badger setts. Before we start, I explain that they have a choice. We can take them on a gentler walk to look at the scenic views – or on a more strenuous trek into the forest to see the badger setts, in which case all the children will have to do exactly as I tell them when we reach the badger area. They all opt for the badger walk, the men telling me that they will carry the elderly ladies if this is necessary and the women assuring me that their children will do as I tell them. Peter acts as sheepdog, keeping the more adventurous children in line.

At the badger setts, I ask the children to queue and I will take them in to see the tunnels three at a time. This is very beautiful. The children treat the setts with reverence, kneeling to extract hairs from the entrances as I show them how. I tell them what the badgers are probably doing now and what will happen at dusk and during the night. Peter has brought some pictures of badgers to show them.

Afterwards we all have a picnic. One poor child is immediately covered with big black ants. I brush her down and distract her by pointing to a dragonfly.

The children call me the badger lady.

19 AUGUST 1984 We are having an economy drive and this means that Keith will sacrifice a morning's photography.

Joe Bussell is draining the sump oil from his Mini when we arrive. The oil is on the garage floor. We all agree it's a problem. Joe Bussell changes the subject: he has news for us! Badgers have attacked a wasps' nest in one of the main clearings on the Reserve. The nest has been excavated – we must go and see. What an amazing sight the badger attack would have been! Here, under the oak, is a hole about 20cm (8″) underground, 33cm (13″) long and 25cm (10″) wide and the paper and tunnels of the nest are clearly exposed. Indignant wasps buzz round us, intent on repair. Keith will return home at once for the cameras and Peter and I will sit in the sun, getting up sometimes to liberate seed from the willowherb and thistles around us. We will make sure no visitors come near the nest and get stung. The kestrel perches near us.

Two women, an elderly lady and a girl in her twenties ask directions. They have come this far into the woods by mistake, looking for a pond which the elderly lady knew in her youth.

'Surely it isn't safe for you here alone?' the younger one asks me – a slight, rather wispy blonde.

'Safe from *what*?' I reply rattily, impatient with female nervousness. The older lady hugs the younger one to her and speaks to me over her head, 'Susan was attacked last year. Badly.' I look into the eyes of the older lady and we understand each other.

'I was thinking of buying a gun so I can go out alone,' said Susan, 'but Gran's been coming out with me, or I borrow a dog. We'll go now, Gran?'

The older lady continues to pass me messages with her eyes and I take the point.

'But you weren't attacked *here*', I say to Susan, touching her arm. 'Stay here with us, let me show you the woods. You don't need a gun if you've got me.' I point to my armband.

This actually makes Susan laugh. Peter, up to now an uneasy witness to the conversation adds loyally, 'My mum knows how to take care of herself.'

I smile my thanks to him, remembering a time when I ventured out clutching his toddler hand in one of my palms and in the other the deadly point of a pair of scissors. I was never attacked badly, like Susan, whose story she tells to me little by little as we walk down the woodland path together – but I can remember what it feels like to be frightened and humiliated and angry.

Peter remains at the wasps' nest and the older lady sits by him in the sun. Susan holds my hand and I choose one of the darker paths. She wants to tell me what had happened to her and I listen, without speaking, pressing her hand more tightly when it seems the right time. We sit down on a little bank, the clearing and wasps' nest a light far at the end of the shady tunnel: Gran and Peter tiny shadow puppets against the sun.

I ask Susan if she feels afraid here and she says that she does not but that now she cannot imagine enjoying walking alone. She wants to go back. Here there are too many shadows. I ask her if she can control her panic and she says she will try.

'Wait for a robin,' I urge her. I explain that I have a theory that in a wood like this, a robin will join anyone in five minutes and I ask her if she will time the five minutes for me because I never wear a watch. Susan agrees and she starts to time the five minutes. Two minutes pass and no robin appears. I hum, explaining that robins like to hear people singing. I show Susan a tormentil and a wood spurge and where a columbine had been – and I curse every robin in this wood!

No robin comes. This is the first time I have ever been ignored by the robins. I tell Susan that it's a rotten time of year for robins. Give it another five minutes. While we wait, I tell Susan about the badgers.

Susan goes to tell her grandmother that she's seen lots of wild flowers and that she will come here again – especially now that she knows it's patrolled by Wardens. I give Susan my telephone number and tell her that I'd love to show her the orchids and the badgers and the nuthatches and the butterflies – and the bluebells. She *has* to come at bluebell time. Everyone has to come at bluebell time. Susan laughs at my enthusiasm, hugs me and says she wishes I was her mother. Her grandmother thanks me and they leave us.

Peter asks me if I'm old enough to be her mother: he's just started Nuffield Biology at school. I am performing the mental calculation when Keith returns with the cameras.

7 OCTOBER 1984 Peter and I warden alone: Keith may join us later. We eat our sandwiches by a badger sett which has many new holes and scratchings and, as summer has gone, no longer smells. Tormentil lines the footpaths still and the woods are dappled and gentle. We find a cluster of earth stars – unearthly fungi beautifully named – and as we kneel to examine them we realise we are also looking at cryptic white signs on the path. Circles with crosses in them. Someone is making a track of some kind with flour or talcum powder. We are curious, but not alarmed. We turn towards the Iron Age Encampment to make sure there is no stupidity going on upon it, and a team of cyclists hurtles past us at top speed. We stand back, amazed.

'What are you going to do?' Peter asks me.

I sigh. 'Follow them and stop them,' I reply.

Following them is easier than I anticipated. They have been forced to stop: the leader of the pack has suffered a puncture. Six other men in their twenties lean on their bikes, bored. The leader is already pink with humiliation. My heart sinks. I turn my armband round so that it shows and approach the group. The leader looks up in challenge. I ask them not to ride in the Nature Reserve as it is against the regulations.

'Why?' asks the leader.

This is actually quite a reasonable question, I think, so I explain.

'Dear God, now *you*' he cries in exasperation, 'we already got mown down by a guy in a landrover on the other side. He told us to stop cycling, too.'

No longer sorry for him, I explain that he obviously met the Forestry Commission Ranger and that there is no cycling on his land either. Roads are for cycling on. Not National Nature Reserves. I stand here, waiting, objectively curious about how we will resolve this. The group looks more alert. This, at least, is giving them entertainment.

'Now, you look like a really nice lady,' the leader begins, 'and me, I'm a really nice guy and I'm sure if we met under any other circumstances . . .' How could he see into my mind so fast? His anger now comes at me like a lash. I am, he tells me, a little Hitler who struts and patronises, an escalating string of unrepeatable obscenities and there is worse to come because I am, he tells me, being unfeminine.

The group are looking uneasy. We would all agree their leader has overdone the swearing. But we have reached deadlock.

'Look,' he starts again, 'if you ask me *nicely* . . .'

I ask for his name and address. His cycling club will be notified by the Resident NCC Warden of the reasons why they must not ride on this land and this will be their official warning. He gives me a name and address and I watch the eyes of the rest of the group to see if he is making up these details. I am surprised to see that he is not. He decides to mend his puncture elsewhere and they push their bikes along the path.

'I bet you they mount up as soon as we've gone,' Peter whispers.

I explain to him that this is not a serious offence but we have to do what the NCC sets down as our duty and I cannot therefore ignore it as, frankly, on a lovely morning like this I would prefer to do.

But trouble is not over yet. Hippies are camping on the Iron Age Camp and clouds of smoke billow up from their inexperienced fire making only yards from the sign which forbids the lighting of fires. I have had enough abuse for one day. Thank God! Keith has arrived and is already arguing with the campers.

A group of runners jog through the wood, chanting rugby songs and raising their fists.

A lot of the fungi is disintegrating into slop.

21 OCTOBER 1984 On arrival in the woods, I immediately challenge a young man who has set up a bright orange tent by the main footpath. Yes, he has permission from the Resident Warden, he assures me. And at 10.30 am there will be 650 more orienteers arriving at the woods. His eyes are glazed with anticipatory bliss and he tells me that this event will be huge.

It is not yet 10 o'clock. We leave the woods at the top of the Reserve and walk down the valley away from the area designated for running. Duck formations fly overhead and we sit in the sun on a bank we decide to name 'bum barrel bank' because long-tailed tits fly in and out of the hazel bushes and bum barrel is their folk name. Mr May of *The Times* likens them to flying spoons and actually this is a better description – but 'flying spoons bank' is somehow inappropriate and doesn't alliterate.

We feel uneasy and know we should be in the running area to keep watch. Peter suggests we go to see if the badger setts are safe from disturbance. We climb back up the Gorge side and discover that the setts are far from safe.

One of the active badger holes – near the largest, most ancient sett in the forest – has been designated an orienteer checkpoint. Badgers change the shape of the terrain – they make little hillocks and excavations – and orienteering maps are models of clarity and detail. A pole is lashed between trees and the orange clipper is dangling over the centre of the hole. It is necessary to stand in the badger hole in order to clip the orienteering card. Runners are already stumbling, jumping, trampling and kicking dirt over the nearby ancient – and still occupied – badger sett. A child competitor is making a point of falling in each hole. I am astonished at the frenzy of these runners. They are in a fantasy – pushing aside everything in their way in their dash between checkpoints.

We are not on our Nature Reserve: we are in the forest. We have no wardening authority here. I try to untie the pole but my hands are shaking. Keith hands me his army knife and I slice through the rope. While I am moving the pole, orienteers are surrounding us like angry wasps, trying to clip their cards. Peter and I want to throw the pole and clipper over the cliff – but Keith explains that the runners will then become even more frantic and damaging in their search for the checkpoint. We move the pole to one side of the sett so that the amount of stomping over the spongey ground is minimised.

An angry, authoritative orienteer is standing in front of me, his face dripping with sweat. He is obviously experienced because he is able to lose precious seconds to ask me what I am doing. He is astounded that anyone should care about a badger sett enough to interfere with a national orienteering event of this size.

'*Badgers?*' he repeats incredulously, raising his hands to heaven, '*Badgers?*'

The orienteer knows he has now lost minutes and belts off, waving his fist and threatening us that we have not heard the last of this . . .

We move on to the next badger sett and find this is worse. Here runners are crawling and tumbling all over the holes. One woman runs three times over the sett to reorientate herself.

I remember with anguish how reverently the children we bring to these setts treat the badgers' homes, tiptoeing carefully, staying for only a few minutes, proud that these wonderful creatures have made their homes here for generations, so close to our city.

10 NOVEMBER 1984 It is dark, wet and cold – and we do not want to go wardening. Throughout the autumn we have faced difficulty, abuse and anger and it is eroding our love of going to the woods. We are at a low ebb. We order a taxi to take us to the Avon Gorge. On arrival, we realise that no one has remembered to wear a watch so we cannot order a taxi back as we will not know the time. We have brought only the minimum food, scratched together in a hurry when we decided we must turf out on patrol – and now we face a walk home. Our spirits sink even lower.

We visit each badger sett in turn and, as we approach the last, we can hear grunts and snuffles under the earth. This revives my passion for what we are doing, and, sitting by the badger sett we discuss what we are going to do to protect the badgers from any further orienteering event. Still angry, Peter and I favour sabotage: Keith is convinced that liaison and discussion could be more effective. He has written to the Nature Conservancy Council, to the leaders of the orienteers and to all local wildlife bodies who might be interested in both the issue of orienteering in woodland Reserves in general, and minimising disturbance at badger setts in particular. We have told our Resident Warden that even though the setts are not on NCC land, we intend to mount guard on them at the next orienteering event.

25 NOVEMBER 1984 We have discovered from the orienteers themselves that there is to be an event in the woods – on both NCC and Forestry Commission land – on March 3rd the following year. By March, the badgers will have cubs in their setts. Keith is going to write about the badgers and the orienteers in *Eye on Local Nature* and he is going to call it *Diary of an Issue*. This is because we are still angry and we need support. Our Warden listens to our plans and tells us that there may indeed be worse problems if we publish the story in our magazine. It will reveal to the public and the press that there are ancient badger setts in the forest. He looks at me and says, 'Poor Mr. Brock the badger. *Everyone* will come and see him . . .' I clench my jaw in anger at this emotional complication and I think he is wrong. We will publish and be damned!

2 DECEMBER 1984 But *now* what has happened? Down in the Avon Gorge there are mountains of litter by the river – polystyrene, road beacons, bottles, tables, old doors . . . These are flanking a quarter of a mile of the tow path and it is a ghastly sight. There is even seaweed massed on the rocks above us. We meet a walker who tells us that there was a freak tide a few days ago and we must wait for the next freak tide to remove all this debris.

We perch on a rock out of the punishing wind and drink our tea. A man walks casually past us with a rifle with a telescopic sight. He is followed by two others with guns and a grotty grey dog which Keith says is a lurcher. They see us and change direction. Before I can stop him, Peter leaps down and runs noiselessly after them. I follow him. A dalliance begins. We have no authority here – this part of the Avon Gorge belongs to British Rail – but we do not like the look of this and are prepared to bluff to stop whatever it is they plan to do. Everytime we confront them and walk across their path, they change directions. We realise that they want to enter a part of the Gorge which is rich in wildlife and precious to us. We sit like a barrier in front of the entrance and freeze in the bitter cold wind. Eventually they disappear out of sight.

We climb the Gorge to go home. At the top of it we are back on the Nature Reserve and here are four men with a rope and an axe. The rope is already slung around a tree and it looks for all the world like a hanging party. No it is not, because they explain to us cheerfully that they have come to practise climbing. We explain that this is a National Nature Reserve and they are surprisingly apologetic. We walk off the Reserve together.

20 JANUARY 1985 Deep, deep snow. The weather reports have threatened the worst snow for forty years. This did not happen, but the snow is packed and deep. Joe Bussell and Cecil Baker are leaning on Joe's gate as we arrive. They tell us that this is not a patch on the winter of 1918. That was the year, Cecil tells us, that he filled many sacks with birds frozen to death on the branches.

The badger pawprints are so textbook clear that we are spoiled for choice as to which to photograph. We can follow their tracks exactly down the badger paths. The snow is like thick lace on the conifers and I am in love with the woods again.

This morning another letter arrived from an *Eye on Local Nature* reader wishing us well in our campaign against the orienteers. We have had many offers of help – even extra money sent to the magazine 'for caring'. We have suggested to the NCC and the orienteers that the badger setts be taped off and marked as no-go areas. Our Warden has agreed to investigate this for us but we must understand that the setts are on Forestry Commission land – they are not on the Nature Reserve – and we have no authority on Forestry Commission land. Relationships between the NCC and the Forestry Commission can be delicate. Nevertheless, we feel this is of little relevance to the badgers.

We stop on the way home to throw snowballs off the suspension bridge.

27 JANUARY 1985 Michael telephones us from the woods! There is now to be action on the badger setts. He acknowledges us as the authorities on the forest badgers and asks if we would accompany him to show him each sett and tell him what we know of its occupation. Keith agrees to go at once. What is behind this wonderful change?

The Forestry Commission has agreed that our NCC Warden can take a watching brief on the badger setts on their land, and, with this permission, Michael is entering into the spirit of the thing with us! We have, in fact, received a letter from one of the orienteer organisers who has agreed with our point of view and raised it in committee. We are now very close to the next orienteering event which is not a large affair as it is the Avon Schools Event. We will have the chance to see if co-operation with the orienteers is possible.

3 FEBRUARY 1985   Peter is on a school trip again. Keith and I try another route from the top of the Avon Gorge to the bottom. We fight through brambles and nettles to a hidden bank halfway down the cliff. Brimstone butterflies flap lazy paths around us. Huge, vivid yellow and tropical these butterflies are out of place here.

Over the river, the gulls are displaying their flying skills. They fall like dead leaves and then swoop up again seconds before they touch the water. We have never seen this before.

I have heard tell of a cave under the cliff at Kestrel Corner and tell Keith I will find it for us. We thrash through more brambles towards a black hole under the cliff. Water is running down the cliff face although it is not raining. It's a dark, dank corner and I stop in horror. I am face to face with a totem pole. We have become used to finding druid-like arrangements of boulders impossible for us to move – but somebody did – and we are used to finding encoded carvings and cryptic paintings on the rocks. But this is bizarre. What does it mean?

Keith investigates. I hold back, spooked. He explains that the ghastly arrangement of poles, driftwood and what looks like a painted face is, he thinks, part of a bivouac. Leaning against the pole is a construction of branches and fresh ivy. The kestrel circles above us, outraged and the voodoo bivouac gives us all the evil eye.

Noting that someone has painted yet another silly face on the rock face (there is a large tin of white pain left underneath it) – we head for the badger setts for some light relief. I investigate each badger hole, looking for signs of activity. In one of the holes a badger has died and its rear is poking out of the hole. There's no smell, no visible maggot movement. The fur is thin and pale. We presume it died of old age. What shall we do? The corpse is stuck too far down the hole for us to pull it up by its tail – and digging at a badger sett is illegal. Keith wants to fill in the hole and bury the creature. I would like to see the body but will not press the point.

The Ministry of Agriculture and Fisheries wants badger corpses as part of their investigations into bovine TB. We leave the body, mark the hole with a stick and report the corpse to the Resident Warden.

We agree that there is no evidence of foul play and that it is unlikely that anyone would kill a badger and then stuff it back down the hole. However, it seems an odd position in which to find the creature and our Warden agrees to investigate and dig the corpse up when he has had his Sunday lunch. No, he does not want our help to paint the new silly face off the cliff slope: it is too dangerous.

27 FEBRUARY 1985 Keith has received a reprimand from the Nature Conservancy Council for the militant tone of his *Diary of an Issue* in *Eye on Local Nature*. It is felt that we are inviting people to go along to face an enemy in the same way that hunt saboteurs go along to the local meet. Confrontation is taboo.

Six hours after we receive the reproving letter from the NCC, the Chief Forester for the Region telephones us for the first time. He is a badger man and cares that the Avon Gorge badgers are left alone. In future, orienteers can run in the forest only if their routes avoid the setts. He wishes us luck, tell us he admires our efforts, asks to be a subscriber to *Eye on Local Nature* and requests a full report from us to the Forestry Commission of what happens at the Orienteering Event on his land.

3 MARCH 1985 The orienteers have set up stall like a jumble sale on the Reserve. There are vast cannisters of orange juice and plastic stickers. We arrive early and visit each badger sett. Every one has been impressively taped off with 5"-wide yellow plastic tape upon which is printed: CAUTION: ELECTRIC CABLE BELOW. Keith stays on guard at one sett, Peter and I at another. Our Warden and his wife patrol the setts in the apple green NCC van.

A robin circles us, perching on the tape. We have been waiting an age in eerie silence. I am starving and eat my sandwiches and Peter's as well. But now they are coming! However, it is only three teenagers who clomp wearily towards us. They see the tape and react as if stung.

'I ain't going in *there*,' we overhear one mutter, 'there's badger traps in there . . .'

Peter and I smile at each other. Then the teenagers return, spread their map out in front of me and plead, '*Please*, tell us where the bloody hell we are?'

Now more runners hurtle past us and no-one comes near the setts. They have been well briefed to keep away from the yellow tape. But now, one orienteer is actually stopping as soon as he sees the tape! He is a chubby little boy, about 8, in a padded anorak, accompanied by his parents. He walks up to the tape and holds it, looking in.

'Are you *allowed* in there?' he asks me.

'Yes, I am,' I reply and start to explain but he cuts across me, 'Why – do you work for the badgers?'

I nod, 'Yes, my love, I do'.

The event is over. We drink orange juice with the organisers who are anxious to please and be reassured. Did they keep away from the badgers? Was everything in order?

Our Resident Warden is excited: he believes this may be a national precedent for badger sett protection in this kind of event.

I am so happy that I cycle back over the Clifton Suspension Bridge singing. Halfway across a large official extends his hand and makes me stop the bike. He asks me if I can read and we agree that I can. He tells me to go back and read the CYCLISTS ARE TO WALK notice at the entrance to the bridge. I refuse to let this spoil my mood.

18 MARCH 1985 The Forester has asked us to give him unofficial general reports on what happens to the flowers and wildlife in his forest. I am overjoyed because I love the Forestry Commission land.

18 MAY 1985 Keith and Peter are photographing the fragile and rare angular solomon's seal. There are supposedly only these few plants. I start to climb the rocks, higher and higher. It is hard going. But now I can call out to them that it's not true – those aren't the only plants left. High up here, where no-one can see, there are hundreds of the rare plants – too many to count – hundreds, hundreds! Paradise regained.

19 MAY 1985 Peter is spending the day in bed reading comics. Joe Bussell is feeding Whitey as Keith and I arrive. Mrs Bussell tells us that this spring she tried to grow 10 busy lizzie seeds. All 10 germi-

nated and grew into 9 stinging nettles and a groundsel. Joe took them back to the shop.

The Conservation Volunteers are in the woods today, looking murderous and remaking a wall. Our Resident Warden tells us that there is more painting on the cliffs. It says 'Simon 4 Karen' and yet again there is a silly face. He is going to paint it off today, or he may put it off until later in the week. This job depresses him. I understand. Vandalism is always depressing.

'We'll do it *now!*' I volunteer, 'won't we Keith?'. Keith nods, though less enthusiastically. Michael looks at me for a long time. He has never let us do this job before because it is too dangerous. This time, however, he agrees. The paint – terrible, adhesive, mud-coloured stuff – is already mixed. Michael will take us to the cliff in his van. We squeeze in and Keith is sitting in the back on a pile of boulders to be taken to the Conservation Volunteers. Mud-coloured paint slops over Keith and the back of the van. We stop at the top of the Avon Gorge cliffs and I show Michael the twin-headed anemone I found.

I ask Michael how we are going to get down the sharp cliff to the slope where the painting is? There is a long drop from the top to where the slope begins. We had expected Michael to take the van around to the bottom of the cliff and to climb up – this being the usual route. Michael pulls paint, brushes and gloves out of the van and gives me one of his old green sweaters to put over my blouse. He tells us that we now have to walk down a thin ledge first and this will take us to the top of the slope. But I know about that ledge – it's the one part of the Gorge Keith thinks is too dangerous for us and we therefore never include it on one of our cliff climbs. Keith holds my wrist, 'No. Don't be a fool. It's crazy – look at that drop.' Michael has already eased himself down onto the ledge. He expects us to follow. Keith, encumbranced by his rucksack, heavy walking boots and a sure knowledge that he will fall to his death, will not come. I look down and wince. I tell Keith I'll be O.K. and slither down onto the ledge. Keith is always more daring than I am and I expect him to change his mind and follow me. When he does not, I am very frightened. I run along the sloping ledge too quickly to take in what I am doing. I catch up Michael, take the paint tin from him and go into the lead. I start to edge down the slope, high above the river and find that it is steeper than I had expected. Michael congratulates me on my sure-footedness and asks me if I do this sort of thing all the time – rock climbing and stuff?

I shake my head and tell him that even so, I'm enjoying it and I'm grateful to him for the opportunity. He shows me a rare plant which we agree is rather dull, despise its rarity.

Michael tells me he is tired: last night he listened to three hours of Wagner and now it is beginning to tell. I know that Michael's job – though enviable – has a tougher side and his is a 24-hour responsibility for the Reserve.

I carry on and paint out 'Simon 4 Karen' and the silly face. The paint is fast-drying, and the brush ancient and hairless. I become skilled at avoiding getting paint under my feet because I cannot risk a slip. My legs are wobbly and I have to concentrate on every movement.

At last Keith reappears. He has found a safer route down the cliff and is now climbing back up the slope towards me. He tells me again that I am a fool, but adds a rather gruff acknowledgement of my bravery. I tell him I was just showing off.

26 MAY 1985 It is the 150th anniversary of the Great Western Railway and steam trains are running on the re-opened line between Bristol and Portishead, along the bottom of the Nature Reserve. Michael is waiting for us by Joe Bussell's cottage – because yet *again* there is graffiti. A list of names painted in huge white letters on the rockface. The train will come through the tunnel soon and as the passengers blink in the light, their vision will clear to see this new vandalism. It is an affront to the pride of his Reserve. Will we all go with him to paint over the names?

We climb up the rock face to the graffiti. Michael watches over Peter for me while Keith takes photographs. Enjoying the urgency, we brush brown paint over the white slogans and collapse, exhausted and laughing when we hear the train whistle and chug out of the tunnel.

Michael tells us he has taken a party of blind people around the badger sett by the cowslip earlier in the week. He will write about it for Peter's magazine. A sand dredger sails up the Avon. We sit together and drink tea, high up, on top of our world.

Conclusion
IN EVERY CITY . . .

How dull our family life would have been without Peter's early love of Nature! What we would have missed! The conservation movement, gathering momentum and power, reaching out, might still have passed us by. Now, as part of the movement ourselves, our concern is to share the generosity and opportunities given to us. Keith and Peter have taken from me the lead in bringing the beauties of the woods to those who have not seen them – their photographs form the popular *Eye On Local Nature* Roadshow. Peter has just begun his radio talks telling families what to look out for in the city and farther afield. The boys' magazine continues to reach new readers. I have returned to my beloved background role of observer, wanderer in the woods, searcher.

I believe our kind of absorption with Nature is possible for most city families. Persistence is the key: visiting one tiny green area time after time until you know it so well you regard it as yours to watch over and protect. Would a garden do? I'm not sure. As city flat-dwellers, we had no garden and I believe this worked to our advantage. We found our clump a little way from home and the expeditions had a safari atmosphere I'd find hard to feel in the back garden with the possibility of the telephone ringing. Also, sitting in our clump to the amusement of the passers-by accustomed us to the occasional raised-eyebrow stares which those engaged in some of the peculiarities of Nature study (lying in the middle of a footpath to take a photograph!) attract.

Wherever I go, in every city and town, my eyes search for clumps: London is especially well-endowed. But can everyone find a clump nearby? Two years ago I was returning from work through a derelict, uncompromisingly bleak part of the city. No chance of a clump here, I thought. I'm wrong, clumps aren't all around us – perhaps I've been wrong all along, perhaps none of our adventures could happen to anyone else. I sat on a wall and disciplined myself to look beyond looking to see what the possibilities were. Pigeons and a few dandelions. I looked up from the pavement and focused on a bush in a school yard. The bush was a mass of shaking leaves and two workmen were

171

sitting by it on the school wall. I moved within earshot. The bush was alive with sparrows and the men were feeding them, encouraging each sparrow by name, 'Bullseye, Scrapper, Bighead.'

Seeing me, the men explained they often came here to feed the sparrows and it was surprising what you could learn about the way sparrows carried on! A pied wagtail joined us, seagulls circled overhead, persian speedwell nestled in the scraps of grass at our feet . . .

Throughout this country, in every city, there are thousands of clumps – the beginnings of adventures and friendships. The beginning of a realisation of how very beautiful this portion of our planet can be – and the beginning of a determination to care for it.

Please, shut this book and find your clump.

APPENDICES

Magazine production

Eye On Local Nature magazine has been running every month since April 1982. It has a circulation of over 100 and is read regularly by many experts in the conservation field. It has raised money for conservation; it has publicised national wildlife issues and fought local ones. It has put us in touch with a great many valued friends: 90 people have written for us. This is why we believe that anyone who is interested in natural history should run a magazine!

In the following pages we show you how to make your own magazine like *Eye On* using the latest techniques. For convenience, we have split the advice into two sections. The first section contains all the techniques needed for making a one-page news sheet – which is a good jumping off point if you haven't produced a magazine before. The second section covers the extra techniques required to produce a full magazine like *Eye on Local Nature*.

Paper sizes
Both the news sheet and the magazine use one size of paper – A4, $11\frac{3}{4}''$ × $8\frac{1}{4}''$ wide (297mm × 210mm). A4 is the standard international (ISO) size for office typing paper and it will fit all typewriters and all photocopiers. All stationers sell it. Right at the start of making a magazine or a news sheet, you will need a large supply of good quality white A4 paper. Get a fairly heavy grade (ask for 80 or 85 gsm) to withstand alterations, rubbing out etc. You will need at least 30 sheets.

Photocopying
The best method for printing short news sheet/magazine runs (up to 150 copies) is photocopying. This is usually cheaper and quicker than real printing because there are no set-up costs and no delays while waiting for the ink to dry. If you are very lucky you may even persuade a friend with access to a machine to run you off some copies free!

PRODUCING A NEWS SHEET

If you haven't made a magazine before, try a news sheet first. This is just one sheet of A4 paper with your news typed or written on one side only and then photocopied. It is simple to produce but it involves most of the techniques you need to know to make a full magazine.

Making the master

The first stage in producing your news sheet is to prepare an original or 'master copy' of it. This 'master' is an exact, same-sized version of what you want to print, complete in every detail. The master is then used on a photocopier to print the news sheet. Start by taking a clean sheet of white A4 paper. Before writing or typing anything on it, you must decide how much clear space (or 'margin') you want to leave round the edges of the page. Look at any page in this book to see what I mean. Get a pale blue coloured pencil and a ruler, and draw in guide lines ('guide margins') to show where the margin starts – on both sides and at the top and bottom of the page. Use one side of the paper only. Remember to leave extra space at the top of the page for the name of your news sheet. Most photocopiers won't print (or 'pick up') pale blue, so these guide margins won't appear on the photocopied sheets.

All the written material (the 'text') is then written or typed onto the sheet inside these margins. Spaces can be left for drawings etc (the 'illustrations') to be added later.

Typewriting techniques

Some children may prefer to handwrite their news sheet, but typewriting does look more professional. If you are not familiar with typewriters, ask a friend who can type to explain about them, especially the use of single and double spacing, and how to set the margin stops. Try to keep all the typing within the blue guide margins you have drawn so that the text forms a tidy block. On the right hand side, some words will run over into the margin. This doesn't matter, but consider splitting long words that are getting too close to the edge of the paper.

When typing the master, remember to:

☐ Use a new, well-inked black ribbon on your typewriter. An old, 'grey' ribbon is a false economy as it will not photocopy well. Also, avoid those black/red ribbons supplied with some machines. They have a nasty habit of slipping and giving striped letters which don't copy well.

☐ If you make a mistake in the typing (or drawing), don't re-do it unless it is a hopeless mess. Use a quick drying white correction fluid like Tipp-Ex. Paint carefully over the error with the brush in the cap, wait for the fluid to dry *completely*, and then type or draw over the top of it. The Tipp-Ex won't show up on the photocopies provided it isn't lumpy.

Filling the page

Before you start to type, decide which articles must be included, and which could be left for a future issue if you run out of space. Then count all the words in the vital articles, adding about 100 words for the 'editorial'. (This is where you can tell readers about the news sheet and your plans for it – give your address, and appeal for their help!) Aim for about 500 words to fill one page of A4 at single spacing on the typewriter. I suggest that you start with the editorial at the head of the page and then follow on with the other items. If you are lucky, they will just fit; but don't worry if you have to run onto an extra line below the bottom guide margin to get everything in.

If you have too many articles, consider these ideas:

☐ Carry articles over to the next issue (tell the contributors that their articles *are* coming up soon).

☐ Serialise one of the longer articles (using *to be continued* . . . at the end of the first instalment).

☐ Unobtrusively shorten some of the articles.

If you are short of articles:

☐ Use double spacing for at least some of the articles.

☐ Increase the spaces left between articles.

☐ Expand the editorial: write about what is coming up in future issues and what you hope the news sheet will achieve.

You will soon be able to judge what will fit – and will acquire valuable experience in how to plan a page.

Layout techniques

'Layout' is the technical term used to cover all the techniques used in newspapers and magazines to present the text and illustrations in a way that is eye-catching and makes you *want* to read it.

The aim of good layout is to hold the reader's eye right down the page, by breaking up the text into easily read portions and by introducing as much visual variety as possible.

Have a look at the various sample pages from *Eye on Local Nature* reproduced in this book, and try using the following *Eye On* techniques in preparing your news sheet.

☐ Keep the articles fairly short. For a one page A4 news sheet, aim for an average of about 100 words for each article so that you can cover several different topics on the one page.

☐ Break down the articles into paragraphs and keep the paragraphs as short as possible to break up the text.

☐ If space allows – use double spacing for one or two items – for variety.

☐ Either leave a gap equivalent to one line of typing between paragraphs or inset the first word of each paragraph by about 5 letter spaces.

☐ Give each article a 'headline', with CAPITAL LETTERS for the name of the article. Underline the whole headline for effect.

☐ Leave a gap equivalent to 2 or 3 lines of typing between items. Then draw a line across the page between the items to separate them and break up the page.

☐ Try to get a variety of written styles into the page – include speech for impact – eg by quoting from readers' letters. Write at least some of the articles in the first person.

☐ Vary your punctuation. Try using dashes (–) instead of commas and brackets. Ask questions and make limited use of exclamation marks and underlining for emphasis.

A combination of these techniques will make your news sheet more compelling to look at and easier to 'dip' into.

Illustrations

Try to incorporate some illustrations (drawings). Readers like them and they make the news sheet more attractive to look at. For the best results, draw these directly onto the master in black biro or even better, Indian ink (black drawing ink). We use 'Rotring' drawing office pens, sizes 0.2mm, 0.4mm and 0.6mm. These are a type of Indian ink pen with a self-contained ink supply in a refillable cartridge. They are easy to use, but dry out very quickly if neglected. The nibs are actually small tubes down which the ink flows. They bend easily, so need very gentle handling. After you have used them, wash them out and put them somewhere safe!

The easiest way to put an illustration into a page of typing is to work out first how big you want the illustration to be. Then, using the pale blue coloured pencil again, mark off on the page a space slightly larger than your intended illustration. Type up the sheet, typing round the space – and then draw in the illustration.

Draw a title

Incorporate the name of your news sheet into an eye-catching title design at the head of the page. If you are artistic, you can draw a title as Matt did for *Eye on Local Nature*. Otherwise you can try one of the brands of black 'dry transfer' (rub-down) lettering that are easy to use and give a professional finish.

Proofing the master

Before printing your news sheet, you should 'proof read' (check) the master to pick up any errors, and correct them at this stage. I recently had to alter 100 copies of *Eye On* by hand, because I had put the wrong issue number on it!

Photocopy printing

Printing the news sheet is simplicity itself! Any photocopier will take your master because it is the standard international office paper size – A4. Hopefully this will mean that you might be able to get office friends to run off a few free. Schools might help, too.

If you have to use a photocopy shop (and we do), it pays to shop around because prices and quality vary considerably. Usually, they charge less per copy the more you have run off, so always print at least ten more news sheets than you think you are going to need, so that you won't run out and have to get the extra sheets printed at the top price. You will certainly need lots of spare copies, not only for reference but also to send out when canvassing prospective contributors and subscribers, and for publicity.

You can also use your master to have your news sheet printed properly, for example on an offset litho printing machine, but unless you intend to print at least 150 copies, it is cheaper and a lot quicker to photocopy it.

Finally – masters are valuable. Make sure that the photocopy shop returns your master to you. They often put it on top of the photo-copied sheets, so be careful not to give it out by mistake! We keep our masters in a separate file inside clear fronted envelopes to keep them clean.

Keep a stock of 'back numbers' (previous issues of the news sheet). Who knows – they may become collector's items. *Eye on Local Nature*'s early issues are now much in demand by readers completing their sets!

A FULL MAGAZINE

As soon as you are regularly getting enough articles to fill a second page of your news sheet, it's time to move on to producing a full magazine. The rest of this section shows you how to use the simple, flexible and economic 'format' (design) that we have developed for *Eye on Local Nature* magazine.

A5 Magazine format

Eye on Local Nature is printed on two sheets of A4 paper which are turned sideways, folded once, slipped inside one another and stapled to make an 8-page magazine. Each sheet of A4 actually has 4 pages printed on it, two on each side. Each of these pages is $8\frac{1}{4}'' \times 5\frac{7}{8}''$ wide (210mm × 148mm) as is the whole magazine, when folded. This corresponds to the international (ISO) paper size A5 (the larger the 'A' number, the smaller the paper). It is exactly half the area of A4.

Fold a sheet of blank A4 in half like a birthday card to get the feel of the new format. Take a second sheet of A4, fold it in half and insert it inside the first sheet – you now have a 'mock-up' (trial copy) of the magazine! Write the page numbers on each page in the right order, starting with the front page 'front cover' (which does not have a number) and continuing 2, 3, 4, 5, 6, 7, 8. Keep this mock-up as a guide for when you put your masters together for final printing.

Making the page masters

As before, each page has a separate master ('page master'), but this time the masters will be on A5 paper. You can either buy ready cut white A5 paper or carefully cut A4 sheets in half using a steel ruler and a sharp knife on a cutting board. Work out the margins you will need round the pages and mark these up on sheets of A5 in pale blue coloured pencil. Altogether, you will need eight A5 page masters – including one for the front cover. Type or write out the text and add illustrations in the usual way.

Appendices

Special production techniques
All the main techniques needed to make the magazine have already
been discussed in the section on news sheets, but we have found the
following helpful to keep in mind.

☐ Each page of the magazine will hold a maximum of 300 words typed single
   spaced.

☐ Make some of the articles a little longer than on the news sheet – eg 300-400
   words, but remember to keep the paragraphs short to break up the text.

☐ Illustrations can be done on separate sheets of paper, cut out with scissors,
   and then stuck into place in the text after typing. Take great care to ensure
   that all the paper edges are firmly stuck down. Check the finished page on
   the photocopier you are using – some copiers are a bit sensitive to paper
   edges (which show up as black lines on the photocopy). If the magazine is
   printed properly, you can use these 'paste-up' techniques with no risk of
   edges showing.

☐ If the illustrations supplied by your contributors are the wrong size,
   consult your photocopy shop. The latest generation of photocopiers have a
   facility to enlarge or reduce by exactly the amount you require within
   certain limits. When you have got the size right, cut the illustration off the
   photocopy and stick it onto the master.

☐ Avoid water-based adhesives, especially for paste-ups because they make
   the paper ruckle and stretch. UHU is good but very quick drying. We use
   3M's Spraymount (in aerosols) – it dries more slowly and sticks right up to
   the edges of the paper. It is expensive, however, and only worth buying if
   you have a lot of paste-ups to do.

☐ A full page front cover is worth the effort. Don't delay doing the cover
   until the last minute, as there is a temptation to skimp it. The cover is the
   ambassador of your magazine.

☐ We use the same title design for *Eye on Local Nature* covers each month,
   and then design the rest of the cover around the illustration of the month.
   The vital information which must always appear on the cover is the issue
   number, the date and the price.

☐ It is useful to number the pages! You can type the numbers on, or use one
   of the dry transfer sheets with numbers only which are made by Letraset
   etc.

Assembling the printing masters
When it comes to assembling the masters ready for printing, a new
technique is needed. The individual A5 page masters go side by side in

181

pairs to make the 'printing masters' (ie the master sheets from which the magazine is actually printed). To get the pages in the right order, take your magazine mock-up apart and refer to the order of the pages on each A4 sheet. Stick the A5 page masters side by side in the same positions on a stiff sheet of A4 (turned sideways), butting the centre edges tightly together and lining up the other edges with the edges of the A4 sheet. Turn the sheet over and do the same on the back with the next two page masters, taking care to keep all the pages the same way up (front and back). Repeat this for the four remaining pages.

The two printing masters are now ready for double-sided photo-copying onto A4 paper.

It is vital at this stage to run a full, double-sided 'proof copy' from the masters (ie a preliminary photocopy of the magazine), to check that all the pages are in the right order and the right way up!

Printing the magazine

The key to producing the magazine is the ability of certain modern photocopy machines to copy onto both sides of a sheet of paper ('double-sided photocopying'). Some office photocopiers have a special button for double-sided photocopying, but this is probably a job for the experts. Most large photocopy shops are set up to do double-sided photocopying – just ask for each master to be photo-copied double-sided the required number of times.

Finishing the magazine

'Finishing' is the term that printers use for all the jobs like folding, collating and stapling that are required to turn the printed pages into a magazine. Most printers and many photocopy shops will do this for you, but it is expensive. It is not difficult to do it yourself.

First split the printed pages into two separate piles containing the inner and outer sections of the magazine. Then fold all the sheets in each section with a single fold across the middle, keeping them in separate piles. Refer to your mock-up magazine to make sure you fold the pages the right way (ie pages 2 & 7 and 4 & 5 are on the inside). Then 'collate' them (ie put them in the right order) by inserting the inners into the outers ready for stapling.

The magazine is 'saddle stitched' – that is, staples are driven through the fold in the magazine, from the outside to the inside, and then bent over inside to hold the magazine together. Most office staplers are too short to reach across to the central fold, so try to borrow a 'long arm' stapler with a reach of at least 6″ (15 cm). Open the magazine out, cover upwards. Put two staples through the magazine fold, in line with the fold and about $1\frac{1}{2}″$ (4cm) in from each edge, then fold the magazine shut.

Your magazine is now ready for distribution and you will find that production gets easier with every issue!

Post script

A small magazine like *Eye On*, with strong local roots has a lot to offer the community. At a local level it is possible to be truly democratic and involve everyone in reporting for the magazine. Our *Eye On* post contains everything from two-line letters from school children to four-page scientific treatises from university lecturers! All are valued, and they all find their way into the magazine.

Nature photography

Every time you open a Nature magazine and see a stunning photograph, whether it's of a tiger, an orchid, a kingfisher or a butterfly – you can be quite certain that it was taken with an SLR camera! The modern 35mm SLR is the basic tool of all wildlife photographers, amateur and professional, and there is a bewildering range of them available.

If you have never bought an SLR before, read these guidelines before spending any money:

☐ Avoid second-hand cameras and buy the best new camera you can afford. Too many things can go wrong with a second-hand SLR, and repairs are slow and very expensive.

☐ Buy from a local dealer so that if you have to return the camera under the guarantee there are no delays.

☐ Almost any SLR will take good wildlife pictures with the addition of the right lenses and accessories. Which camera you chose depends on what else you want it to do – discuss this with your local dealer.

☐ It is sound practice to chose a camera made by one of the major optical manufacturers – Praktica, Olympus, Pentax, Minolta, Canon, Nikon etc, even if you have to go for a 'bottom of the range' (basic) model. The lenses supplied with these cameras should be of a very high standard and will usually be the same as those used on the higher-priced models. This leaves you free to upgrade the rest of the camera (the body) when you can afford it. Keep the original camera body as a 'back up' (spare). Generally speaking, the range of lenses and accessories available for the 'big name' cameras is wider and better.

☐ To make sure you are getting a good deal on the price, get an up-to-date copy of *Amateur Photographer*. This magazine comes out weekly and all the equipment suppliers advertise in it. This will help you to get an idea of what the current discount price is for particular cameras.

☐ Each week, *Amateur Photographer* prints a very useful checklist of SLR cameras, with all the models in each price range listed with 'star ratings' for value and performance. Don't buy anything with less than a 3-star rating on both counts. Another useful source of information on cameras is *Which?* magazine which reviews SLRs every couple of years.

☐ Reviews of cameras are coming out every week in the various photographic magazines. If you can wait before buying your camera, read the reviews of different cameras to familiarise yourself with the terminology and the facilities offered. You can usually get back copies of reviews of a particular camera for a small fee. Write direct to the magazine concerned.

When you have got your camera and mastered using the controls, turn your attention to getting the best deal with film and processing. A word of warning – some cheap or 'free' colour films are of very poor standard. Use the big names, eg Kodak, Fuji or Agfa, and concentrate on getting these at discount prices. Consult *Amateur Photographer* for the best offers.

Processing (ie developing and printing) is a complex area. You can pay widely differing prices depending on what you want. The only dependable bargains are the postal offers by the various bulk processing laboratories. *Which?* and the photographic magazines check these out fairly regularly, so watch out for articles on the best offers. The bulk processors offer one of two standard sizes of colour print for 35mm films: enprints $5'' \times 3\frac{1}{2}''$ (127mm × 89mm) and jumbo prints $6'' \times 4''$ (152mm × 102mm). The moment you move away from these sizes, the prices increase sharply.

A word about black and white photography. Unless you do your own processing, black and white photographs will cost you at least as much as colour, such are the economies of scale in bulk colour processing. Apart from exhibitions, the only common use of black and white is to make prints for reproducing as 'half tones' (black and white photographs) in magazines and newspapers.

Most people use colour print ('negative') film because it is easier to show the results in albums etc, but for the record, here are the main uses of colour transparencies (slides):

☐ For public shows/lectures/promotions, frequently as part of audio-visual presentations. Colour slides projected onto a large screen carry a lot of clout. The *Eye on Local Nature* Roadshow uses 140 wild flower colour slides and runs for about $1\frac{1}{4}$ hours with commentary.

☐ For scientific record. Colour transparencies give a truer record of the precise colours of flowers for example, especially if electronic flash is used to illuminate the subject.

☐ For reproduction as magazine/book illustrations. Colour printing of photographs needs transparencies not prints. Professional picture agencies do not take colour prints, *only* slides.

Toughening up

The most magical thing in Nature watching is to go out early when there has been a fresh fall of snow and track all the animals by their paw prints, like an Indian Brave. If you are going to last more than a few minutes in these conditions without getting uncomfortably cold and wet, you need to be well fed, well clothed and physically fit!

The aim of toughening up is to increase your efficiency so that:

☐ you can concentrate on Nature watching unaffected by physical distractions such as gnats, nettles, briars, flies and wasps – not to mention mud, wind and water!

☐ you can walk farther without effort and arrive in good condition so that you can make the best use of your time.

☐ you can fit Nature watching in with your other commitments, without needing time off to recover every time you go out!

☐ you can help other people by not getting into difficulties yourself and by being strong enough to help those who do.

The fittest people I know cycle or swim regularly or play a sport or go jogging but if you can't manage these, you can go walking – and you can do this as a family. Combine this with your Nature watching – walk to your clump every week, and gradually go farther and explore new areas. The important part, particularly for children, is to walk hard and climb a few slopes to strengthen your legs and build up stamina. Later on try a few short scrambles up rough (not vertical) slopes – older children love this! Climb up behind them to steady them if they slip. Make them go one at a time for safety. It is wise to have two adults present at all times when taking children out into the countryside. If you intend to scramble up slopes, don't have more than three children to each adult. Avoid cliffs and quarries and rocky shorelines – and leave rock climbing to the experts. Toughening up is also an attitude of mind. It has as much to do with persistence as with physical strength. Visit your favourite area every week throughout the year and try to take the weather in your stride. (A car is a great help here because you have instant shelter as soon as you get back from walking.) Suggestions for winter clothing are at the end of the *Venturing farther* section, and are adequate for lowland walking (under 1000 feet, 300 metres). Hill walking is fabulous but is definitely not for the inexperienced in winter.

One hazard of hill walking that can occur anywhere is 'exposure' (hypothermia). It is a kind of super-chill brought about by getting wet and cold and staying that way for too long. The body starts to lose heat faster than it can produce it, and if the lost heat is not replaced quickly you could actually die of cold. The symptoms of exposure, 'irrational behaviour, stumbling, bad language, chattering, being morose', tend to be vague and could arise from other causes. If you are out in 'exposure' conditions – ie it is cold, wet and windy, and especially if one of your party has got wet or has started shivering violently, take precautions. Change wet clothing for any dry clothing you have with you. Hand out high energy foods like Mars bars, chocolate, etc. Serve hot drinks from your thermos, get people singing, chanting, stamping their feet, wiggling their toes, clapping their hands, waving their arms. Cut short your trip and get back indoors quickly. Read up about the treatment of exposure in outdoor books like the excellent *Spur Book of Survival and Rescue* by Terry Brown and Rob Hunter, published by Warne. This book is required reading for anyone venturing into upland areas for the first time.

Toughening up involves taking and assessing risks on behalf of yourself and other people, including children. As the adult, you are automatically the leader, so here, from our experience, are a few guidelines:

☐ Always eat well before going out as you don't always know how long you will be away! Take plenty of food with you, especially high energy foods like chocolate, glucose sweets, biscuits, Kendal Mint Cake – and even Polos! Take a thermos with enough hot drink for a cupful for everybody.

☐ Always take waterproof clothing including over-trousers. Always take a spare pullover. If you are intending to stay out all day, consider taking a full change of clothes.

☐ Always take a large scale map of the area you are visiting. Ordnance Survey Landranger Maps (scale $1\frac{1}{4}''$ to 1 mile, 2cm to 1km) are ideal and cover a large area on each sheet. Get a compass and learn how to navigate with it.

☐ Always carry a small first aid kit and a first aid manual. If you are leading groups regularly, it's sensible to take a first aid course with St. John's Ambulance or the Red Cross.

☐ In assessing how far to walk, remember that the speed of the party is the speed of its slowest member and with children, this can be as slow as 2 mph (3 km/h). Progress is always slower cross country and up hills. Remember that every mile walked away from the car is really two miles because you will have to walk back!

☐ When planning a walk don't make it too much of an obstacle course. This is particularly important with young children whose energy is limited. Build up gradually so that they enjoy it and leave plenty of time for just looking at things. Post one adult at the rear of the group to encourage stragglers and monitor this closely yourself. If it's obvious that you've been too ambitious, replan the route at once and get everyone back as quickly as possible. Remember it's not a route march!

☐ Always take a torch. In the winter, take two torches, and be careful in the afternoon because on dull days the darkness sets in very quickly. Also, take enough whistles to issue one to every member of the party, so that if anyone gets separated from the group they can call for help. Cover your ears with your hands when using the whistle so that you will be able to hear any response immediately afterwards! At night you can use a torch as well to signal.

☐ As leader, consider taking a large plastic 'survival bag' (purchased from camping shops) and a spare blanket. I also take a length of lightweight climbing rope about 50 ft (15m) long for emergencies.

☐ Check the weather forecast, particularly if you are going somewhere that is a bit exposed. If you are going anywhere near the seashore, check the tides!

☐ Make sure that someone else knows where you've gone, and when you are supposed to be back. If you are going somewhere off the beaten track, leave details of your route, and don't go alone.

Finally, as a leader, never be afraid to act on intuition, especially for safety. If you suddenly get a bad feeling about the weather, or about one of the party who might be vulnerable – however much they protest they are not – don't hesitate and head back to habitation.

Wardening opportunities

The proximity of the Avon Gorge National Nature Reserve to a major city obviously brings special pressures. What wardening is like elsewhere at a minute by minute level depends upon the organisation for which Voluntary Wardens or Rangers are working, the terrain (which could, for example, be upland or coastal) and the nature of the Reserve, Woodland or National Park. There is, too, a variety of 'specialisation' – RSPB Voluntary Wardens protect breeding birds, whereas a group of Voluntary Wardens in the Northumberland National Park have formed themselves into the Fell Rescue Team.

All Park and Reserve wardening requires a sensitive, friendly approach to public relations, an in-depth knowledge of the area patrolled – and the physical fitness to go out in all weathers. The minimum age for acceptance is 18–21 and some training is usually available – many National Parks offering carefully graded and comprehensive training schemes.

Applicants for Nature Conservancy Council and National Park wardening are usually required to serve a probationary period, lasting from 3 months to 1 year and of this requirement, the Chief Ranger of the Peak District National Park comments, 'About 1 in 3 of those who apply successfully finish the course. The probationary period lets the romantics and others drop out without loss of face.'

The NCC is fairly flexible in its time requirement – some areas asking for a patrol round the Reserve 'at least once a month'. The minimum wardening commitment in the National Parks is between 5 and 12 one-day patrols, and the RSPB (applicants 17 and over) asks for a minimum of one week's residential work. The Woodland Trust, acquiring woods all over the country and with a fast increasing wardening team, asks that visits should be made 'as often as possible' and tries to organise rotas of Wardens so that its woods are visited at least once a week. Many Wardens offer far more than the minimum, however, and some travel long distances to reach 'their' Park or Reserve. Working for the NCC, Geraldine and I (with Peter) warden together or alone, and put in fifty 4-hour patrols each year.

Most applicants learn of wardening opportunities by meeting a Warden on duty – as we did! It should be possible to find a Reserve or Park of some kind near you. A starting point is to contact one of these organisations, telling them what you can offer in terms of time and experience, asking them for information and the next step to take.

The Nature Conservancy Council,
Great Britain Headquarters,
Northminster House,
Peterborough, PE1 1UA
0733 40345

The Countryside Commission for Scotland,
Battleby,
Redgorton,
Perth, PH1 3EW
0738 27921

The Council for National Parks,
45 Shelton Street,
London, WC2H 9HJ
01 240 3603

The Woodland Trust,
Autumn Park,
Dysart Road,
Grantham,
Lincolnshire, NG31 6LL
0476 74297

The Royal Society for the Protection of Birds,
The Lodge,
Sandy,
Bedfordshire, SG19 2DL
0767 80551

WATCH

We need to share what we know. My feeling is that the more groups you have time to join – the more information you can share – the better, especially at first. Joining organisations and groups helps you and your children look at lots of possibilities and helps clarify your areas of specialist interest – as well as helping you to understand how they fit into the overall picture. We were joiners before we became initiators.

One of the most exciting developments in family nature involvement is the growth of WATCH. WATCH, a 'club with a difference' is run by an independent educational charity, the Watch Trust for Environmental Education Ltd, which is sponsored by the Society for the Promotion of Nature Conservation and the *Sunday Times*. Through the SPNC it is closely linked to the county Nature Conservation Trusts in the UK and is regarded by them as their junior membership branch. WATCH states that its aims are, 'To open children's eyes to their surroundings, help them to understand the influences which have shaped it and involve them in its future. It is essentially practical, informal and fun and appeals to children as a holiday and spare time interest which may well last them a lifetime.'

Children who join WATCH are involved nationally and locally in campaigns, in setting up mini wildlife reserves in gardens, planting trees and surveying shorelines. Children receive an excellent magazine and, most important of all, the chance to join an active local WATCH group based on a number of families, friends, school – or Conservation Trust local group.

Not only is WATCH worth joining for all children – but it offers adults the chance of WATCH leadership. The back-up material, ideas and enthusiasm of the WATCH organisation is superb – and the opportunities for adventure enormous!

WATCH
22 The Green,
Nettleham,
Lincoln LN2 2NR
0522 752326

Books

STARTING
All our early knowledge, especially Peter's, grew from our own observations and these books:

AA Book of the British Countryside, Drive Publications, 1973.

Wild Flowers of Britain, Reader's Digest, 1981.

Birds of Britain, Reader's Digest, 1981.

Mushrooms and other fungi of Great Britain & Europe, Roger Phillips, Pan, 1981.

The Observer's Book of Wild Animals, Maurice Burton, Frederick Warne, 1971.

A Complete Guide to British Butterflies, Margaret Brooks and Charles Knight, Jonathan Cape, 1982.

The Times Nature Diary, Derwent May, Robson Books, 1983.

REFERENCE
As our interest developed, we turned to these books for reference:

The Wild Flowers of Britain and Northern Europe, Richard Fitter, Alastair Fitter, Marjorie Blamey, Collins, 1974.

The Tree Key, Herbert L Edlin, Frederick Warne, 1978.

The Natural History of the Garden, Michael Chinery, Fontana, 1977.

Wild Flowers of Britain, Roger Phillips, Pan, 1977.

Grasses, Ferns, Mosses & Lichens of Great Britain & Ireland, Roger Phillips, Pan, 1980.

MORE ADVANCED
The New Concise British Flora, W. Keble Martin, Michael Joseph, 1982.

Flora of the British Isles, Clapham Tutin & Warburg, Cambridge University Press, 1962.

FOR INSPIRATION
The Natural History of Selborne, Gilbert White, Penguin, 1977, first published, 1788.

Woodland Plants, Heather & Robin Tanner, Robin Garton, 1982.

White Spirit, Fly Free, One man's fight to save Britain's swans, Pamela Townsend, Sidgwick & Jackson, 1984. (The story of Len Baker, founder of the Swan Rescue Service.)

And everything and anything written by the most passionate and extraordinary genius of the British countryside: Richard Jefferies (1848–1887).

Our favourites are:

The Life of the Fields, Richard Jefferies, first published, 1884, Oxford University Press, 1983.

Field and Hedgerow, Richard Jefferies, first published, 1889, Oxford University Press, 1982.